BELGIAN ALE

PIERRE RAJOTTE

 A Brewers Publications Book

Belgian Ale
By Pierre Rajotte
Classic Beer Style Series
Edited by Ed Yost

ISBN: 0-937381-31-4
Printed in the United States of America
10 9 8 7 6 5 4 3 2

Published by Brewers Publications,
a division of the Association of Brewers, Inc.
PO Box 1679, Boulder, Colorado 80306-1679 USA
(303) 447-0816 • FAX: (303) 447-2825

Direct all inquiries/orders to the above address.

Cover design by Robert L. Schram
Cover photography by Michael Lichter, Michael Lichter Photography.

Table in cover photo courtesy of The Country Cricket, Antiques and Collectibles, Boulder, Colo. Photographs and labels courtesy of Pierre Rajotte, Jérôme Denys, Iain Loe of the Campaign for Real Ale, Chuck Cox, Eric Warner, Leifmans Brewery and Rodenbach Brewery. A special thank you to Walter Lewis of Sabena Belgian World Airlines and Durobor Glassware of Belgium.

Table of Contents

Acknowledgements

I would like to thank the following persons who have contributed directly or indirectly in the preparation of this book.

First and foremost is Joris Van Gheluwe, a retired brewmaster. His encyclopedic knowledge of brewing science, and his generosity in letting me use many references in his extraordinary private library were of utmost importance in preparing the text in its historical perspective. His personal review of the manuscript confersed a seal of authenticity on its content.

Equally important is Jérôme Denys of "Le Cheval Blanc" whose generosity made possible the brewing of some of the recipes, and the conducting of all kinds of weird experiments. He also contributed personally by visiting breweries and taking numerous photographs of establishments that I could not visit.

Alain Fisette of "Les Promotions ZIG-ZAG" (agents for many of the breweries mentioned in this work) contributed by obtaining many technical specifications of beers presently brewed in Belgium, and by presenting the style in its right perspective. His keen sense of tasting was also invaluable.

His partner, Jean-Pierre Leblanc, also made great contributions by obtaining samples for comparison tastings.

Many thanks also to Maurice Renaud formerly internal auditor of Dow Breweries. He was instrumental in procuring my first live brewing yeast a few years ago, when I was on the verge of quitting homebrewing frustrated by the impossibility of obtaining a true beer taste with the ingredients available at that time.

Finally, a big kiss to Lucille, my faithful companion, who encouraged and guided me at every step in the preparation of the manuscripts. She also made a significant contribution in the tastings and evaluation of the beers mentioned in the book.

About the Author

Born in Montreal, Pierre Rajotte obtained a degree in Mechanical Engineering from Ecole Polytechnique in Montreal. Starting his career with the Ford Motor Co. in Dearborn, Mich, he eventually proceeded from heavy trucks to various types of recreational vehicles. He was for many years a franchise dealer of motor vehicles. He eventually sold the business to prove his activity in the field of international automotive consulting. Simultaneously he took up homebrewing. His numerous travels made him an avid taster of beers from around the world. After an assignment on a World Bank contract in Paraguay, he returned to Montreal where he helped a friend (Jérôme Denys) establish the city's first brewpub, "Le Cheval Blanc."

He has contributed articles in the last three Special Issues of ***zymurgy*** and is actively researching the history and evolution of brewing science. He also manufacturers professional quality brewing equipment in the range of one and two barrels. This has lead him to teach brewers ways of improving their techniques by using more sophisticated equipment.

When you ask him to classify his occupation he replies,

"I guess that calling me a brewing coach aptly describes my functions. I am a person that helps good brewers become better brewers."

When you ask him what his favorite Belgian ale is, he replies: "I haven't tasted a bad one yet."

Foreword

This is a useful book. It is reasonably comprehensive, leading the reader from the basics of artisanal brewing technology through the commercial production of various types of Belgian ales. I do not know of any comprehensive book describing with remarkable details and suggestions the production of these types of artisanal specialty ales. Most brewing textbooks are oriented toward the production of lager beers. This textbook is dedicated to the amateur brewers and to professional brewers at small- and medium-size breweries.

The microbrewer, who has to be brewer and bottler, is usually not a scientist but a practician. Numerous descriptions and techniques to improve the production of specialty beers are described. The purpose of this book is to popularize artisanal brewing science. The amateur and the professional alike can consult it with advantage and interest as a guide to choosing raw materials and brewing technique for the production and processing of his products. Therefore, I recommend this useful book to the dedicated amateur and microbrewer of specialty Belgian-type ales and beers.

Joris Van Gheluwe
Retired Master Brewer
Longueil, Province de Québec
Canada

Joris Van Gheluwe is a graduate of brewing science from the Hogere School Voor Gistingsbedrijven in Ghent. He was the director of technical research and development for a major Canadian brewery for more than 30 years. He has published many papers on various aspects of brewing science and holds many patents. He is also a Fellow of the Institute of Brewing, and a member of the Master Brewers Association of the Americas.

Introduction

When you ask people where Belgium is situated most people reply that it is somewhere in Europe close to France and to other countries. When you asked them about Belgian beer, you get answers like: "Oh yeah, those weird, sour, and acid beers," or, "The beer is so strong that you can only drink one." All this is probably due to the fact that Belgians are quiet, unassuming people who like to do their own thing right, and do not brag about it.

Until a few years ago Belgians basically made beers for their own market. But the *Common Market* changed it all. During the 1950s, Brussels became more or less the unofficial capital of Europe. Many corporate headquarters were established there and people from many European nations came to work. The majority of them discovered Belgian beer in all its varieties. Upon returning to their native countries, they talked about it. With the gradual dismantling of tariff barriers, all of Europe suddenly became one large open market for Belgian breweries. Within a few years Belgian beer became fashionable throughout Europe.

Having so many varieties and brands to choose from is confusing, even for experts. Until recently, few Belgian beers made their way across the ocean to North America. Even today, their distribution is very spotty. Beer tasters unaware of what is under the cap can be pleasantly or unpleasantly surprised. The acid tang of an "Old Brown" can be a sheer delight or a taste that you will never like.

Belgium is a country made up of Flemish-speaking people in one area and French-speaking people in another. In some locales, especially around Brussels, the two groups are intermixed but in other areas they do not share any common bonds with their opposite language neighbor. This regional ethnicity is apparent in Belgian beer distribution. Apart from the ever-present Pils, most beers cater to a regional palate, and are unavailable outside the immediate area of a particular brewery. With more than 600 brands on the market at any given time, tasting a small percentage of them is a challenge — tasting all of them is a monumental task.

Surrounded by France to the south, Germany and Luxemburg to the east, and the Netherlands to the north, Belgium has seen many turmoils in its history. It has existed as a nation only since 1830. At various times it has been under Spanish and French rule. However, one thing was always evident — the beer was praised. Situated north of the wine-grape growing area, beer has always been considered the national beverage. Wine imported from France is somewhat popular in the French-speaking Walloon area. But even there beer is the major beverage.

Today, wine-producing and wine-drinking countries such as France and Italy are discovering the numerous tastes available in Belgian beer. Consequently, they are the principal countries to import Belgian beer products.

Belgians themselves are quite keen on imported beer. The finest bottled British pale ales are available in most cafés. These higher gravity brews [between 1.050 (12.5°

Bécasse Rue Tabora, Brussels. Photo by Chuck Cox.

Plato) and 1.070 (17.5° Plato)] are available in both imported and Belgian varieties. Oddly, high quality pale ales made by such breweries as Whitbread and Bass are unavailable in England or, at best, hard to find. They are survivors of the way pale ale was brewed a century ago and are a required tasting for any pale-ale enthusiast visiting Belgium. Once you have tasted Guinness stout brewed for the Belgian market you will really know the meaning of the slogan: "Guinness is good for you."

I first became interested in beers accidentally through my introduction to homebrewing. Until then, beer was something routinely purchased. I knew it was brewed around the world but I had never tasted or experimented with its many varieties. My first encounter with a beer that tasted different from the local Montreal products was homebrewed beer. Immediately, I was hooked, partly because I could have something different, and partly because I could brew it myself. From that moment on, I started to taste every beer I could lay my hands on. Unfortunately, I quickly ran out of steam because at that time there were only about six brands of imported beers available locally.

One day a friend who was a wine fancier invited me to travel with him to Vermont, where he was going to purchase wines unavailable in Montreal. He had previously mentioned that the store had a few imported beers. The store appeared very unassuming from the outside, but upon entering I saw a beer-lover's gold mine: beers from all over the world. Soon I filled the shopping cart, and shortly after, the tasting began. Having never had a beer from Belgium, I first sampled an Orval. What a revelation! I never thought beers could taste like that. Although all the beers tasted that day revealed new tastes, the Orval was the one that impressed me the most. From then on, I was on the lookout for Belgian beers. Wherever I traveled through North America, I was searching. The education came slowly and the courses were few and far between, until one day I accompanied another friend who is an agent for various European breweries on a trip to Belgium.

This was a crash course combining brewery visits, tastings, and talks with brewmasters while sampling their products. The month following that journey I must have brewed 20 times. I used different yeasts acquired in Belgium and tried new methods I learned. Since then I have always brewed with the Belgian philosophy: Try to create something new based on age-old tradition.

People who like to categorize everything in an orderly manner will not feel secure in the way Belgian beers are classified. In some countries strict laws govern the way beer is classified and brewed. In Belgium there are laws too, but they are more guidelines than barriers. With about 100 breweries in a country where you can drive from one end to the other in two to three hours, competition is fierce. Inventiveness is the key to survival. In the chapters that follow I will present an inside look at how Belgian beer was, and is, made so that you can appreciate it and eventually brew it yourself.

The guidelines covered in this book reflect what is actually available on the market in Belgium. The majority of these products are not available in North America, and some may never be. Most of the specifications in this book have a much broader range than what has been previously published. But they reflect data from breweries and suppliers, and allow brewers to brew in a style with the necessary latitude required for inventiveness.

1

History of the Belgian Style

To classify what we might call specific styles of brewing prevalent in Belgium today, we first need to go back to the Middle Ages. The way the brewing art was practiced then and how it evolved is often reflected in the way certain brewers follow centuries-old brewing traditions.

During the Middle Ages brewing was regulated by powerful local brewing guilds. Guilds regulated the composition of the wort and fixed the prices. If the price of raw material increased, they sometimes authorized the brewers to add water to the beer in order to keep its price at the same level. Each city had its brewers making beer unique to the city.

During the 1300s, the ingredients depended on what was available locally. The Flanders region has always grown wheat, so wheat was normally used in the local beer. Oats were also quite common in those times. Barley was used in both malted and unmalted form. Even buckwheat was part of some recipes. During the Middle Ages the popular beer was called *gruitbeer*. At that time hops were not used. Instead a mixture of herbs called *gruit* was used to give aroma and taste to what was basically a sweet product. *Gruit* consisted mainly of sweet gale *(myrica gale)*, sage *(salvia)*, common yarrow *(achillea millefolium)*, and pine *(pinus)* resin. Wormwood *(artemisia absinthium)* and broom *(cytisus)* were also employed. Today adventurous brewers are using these herbs in small quantities to achieve special taste effects.

ADVENT OF HOPS

The use of hops in brewing was unknown to early brewers. Its use first became common around 1000 A.D. in what is today Czechoslovakia. Gradually, hopping spread westward to Germany, and finally made its way to Holland in the late 1300s. The Dutch were beer exporters, and it was hopped Dutch beer that soon became popular in the area that is today known as Belgium. Compared to *gruitbeer,* hopped beer was said to have a much finer taste. More importantly, the use of hops greatly improved the stability of beer.

In the late 14th century, the whole brewing scene changed. Herbs were out and hops were in. At the turn of the 15th century almost all the brewers had changed over to hopped beer. Hops were grown locally wherever there was a brewery. Even nowadays Belgium still produces some hops in small quantities. Since the varieties grown are primarily the bitter ones such as Northern Brewer and Brewers Gold, brewers cannot rely entirely on locally grown hops. The hops imported into Belgium today are primarily from Germany, Czechoslovakia, Yugoslavia and Great Britain.

The basic brewing technique used between 1400 and 1850 A.D. was to make an infusion with either cold or hot water, draw off some of the liquid, boil it and put it back in the mash tank. This was similar to a decoction method but without the grain portion of the mash. This process was repeated quite a few times until the wort was finally drawn.

Not until the late 1800s was sparging practiced. In medieval times, the first wort was drawn off and sent to the brew kettle. This was called a *premier métier* and the resulting beer was always a premium-quality beer reserved for the more fortunate people. It was usually known as a "double." The spent grain still contained sugar, so hot or boiling water was added and the whole mash mixed again. After a suitable rest this second wort (called a *deuxième métier*) was drawn off and sent to either another brew kettle or to the first brew kettle which, by that time, had been emptied out. When the first kettle was used, the same hops were often boiled again. This beer was known as a "simple."

REGIONAL PALATES

Trying to classify Belgian beers in well-defined styles is like attempting to impose guidelines on the Belgian brewmaster's creativity. There are always beers that at one time or another probably started a trend which might be defined as a style. But if you look at the beers included in a so-called style, you will see that a narrow definition is impossible. It would be a barrier to inventiveness.

At the turn of this century, a style was simply a particular way of brewing in a certain community. Thus beers brewed in Antwerp were known as barley beers "Antwerp style." In most cases beer was made with only malted barley but certain brewers were known to add small quantities of wheat and/or oats. The brewing process was long and complicated and usually resulted in two beers being made from the same mash. The first one was a "small beer" with a starting gravity of 1.025 (6.3° Plato). The second was a premium "double" with a starting gravity of 1.055 (13.5° Plato). It was brewed only in winter and the double was known to keep for at least two years.

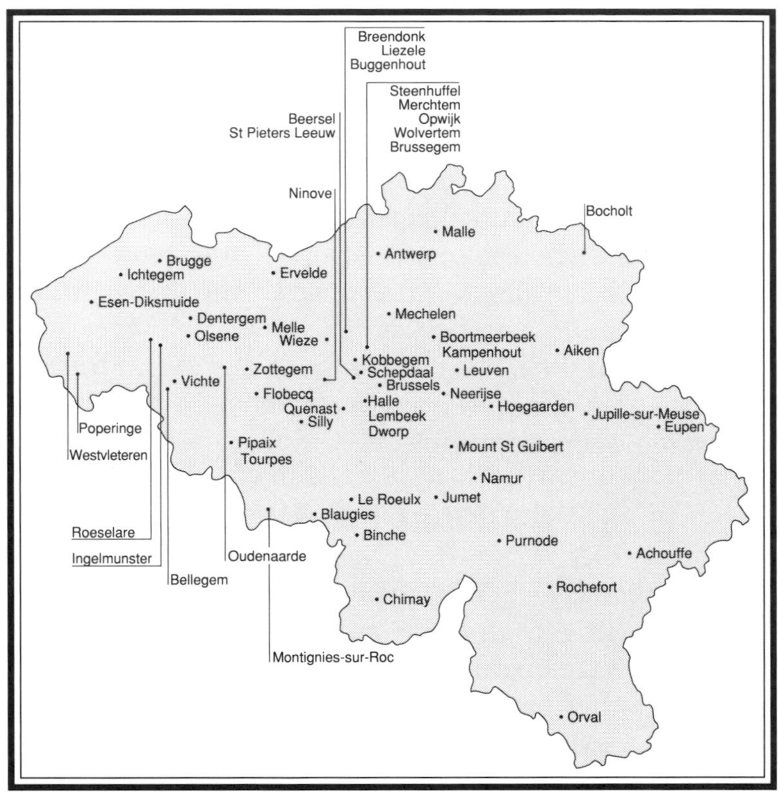

Three different barley-malt beers were brewed in Leuven (Louvain) a century ago. The "March" was a weak beer made with only the last runnings from the mash tank. The malt beer *enkel gerst* was brewed with the middle runnings and the double malt *dobbel gerst* was the result of only the first runnings. The double had a starting gravity of around 1.060 (15° Plato).

In Flanders the predominant brewing style was the *Uytzet*. It was made with malted barley and, at times, a slight addition of raw wheat or oats. It was described as a golden beer with a rich taste that could be also tart and acidic. Here again there was the simple beer with a lower starting gravity and the double with a starting gravity of around 1.060 (15° Plato).

The brown beers of Flanders were also well known. They were brewed like the *Uytzet* but used malt dried at a higher temperature toward the end of the drying cycle. These beers were boiled for 15 to 20 hours to achieve their color and aromas. After a rapid primary fermentation of two to three days, some of these beers were on sale within 15 days. The best ones were fermented slower and sold after two to three months.

The French-speaking province of Hainaut was famous for the quality of its malted barley beers. French-speaking Belgians have always been reluctant to use wheat in brewing. They have preferred a strictly barley-malt beer. Here again it was a current practice to have two beers: the simple and the double. The simple beer was sometimes delivered after seven days but the double was always aged longer.

Despite Hainaut, beers with a high proportion of raw wheat in the mash have always been regarded as a kind of Belgian speciality. Probably the most famous are the spontaneously fermented Lambics, made in the greater Brussels area. Other, equally famous wheat beers have been made in other Flemish-speaking areas.

The Leuven (Louvain) white beer was a well-defined style over a century ago, but has almost completely disappeared. There are white beers brewed today, but they are not brewed as they were at the turn of the century. White beer was meant to be consumed soon after primary fermentation. It was usually on the market four to five days after primary fermentation was complete and consumed during the following two weeks. Any later and it apparently became acidic and sour. However, in the winter, white beer could be kept for up to a month. Bottled in jugs, it was very effervescent and refreshing.

A slight variation in the brewing process of white beer was used for the production of the *Peeterman*. This beer had a generous amount of residual dextrin sugar providing a pleasant honey taste. Like all white beer of that time it was cloudy, white, and very effervescent.

Another famous brewing town was Diest. There the beer was made with 40 percent raw wheat and locally-made barley malt. The regular Diest product had a starting gravity of 1.054 (13.5° Plato) and the double 1.070 (17.5° Plato). A special "Guilde Beer" reportedly had a starting gravity of 1.120 (30° Plato). Sold at auctions, *Guilde Beer* was usually acquired by well-heeled amateurs. A brown beer with a starting gravity of 1.050 (12.5° Plato) was also a local specialty.

A well-appreciated brown beer was also brewed in Mechelen (Malines). It was a mixture of one-third wheat and two-thirds malt. Here again there was a simple and a double. The beer was aged from one to three months before being sold, but with one peculiarity: it was blended with one-third old beer that had been aged from 12 to 18 months. This blend gave it a special old-beer taste. The present-day Gouden Carolus brewed by Het Anker in Mechelen has a taste which I believe reveals that this old blending technique is used in its fabrication.

If the names of all these towns sound unfamiliar, Hoegaarden may ring a bell because a white beer is still made there. Even over a century ago the white beer from Hoegaarden was a very popular, refreshing summer beer. At that time it was brewed with a mixture of one-third raw wheat, one-quarter to one-third raw oats and the balance of malted barley. The brewing method was long and fastidious. One part of the wort was hopped and one part was not. They were cooled separately overnight and mixed the next day in large wooden barrels. It is reported that no yeast was added. The fermentation was slow (10 to 12 days) and the beer was served from the cask while still fermenting. White beer from Hoegaarden was made only in the summer and had to be drunk quickly otherwise it would sour.

The town of Liège was another town known for its bière jeune (young beer). It was a half-and-half mixture of malted barley and raw wheat. Roasted malt was added for coloring. The beer was brewed year-round but was meant to be drunk young. In the winter, *Bière de Saison* was made. This was a high-quality product sold only after aging four to six months. It was hopped with the best Bavarian hops available.

INNOVATION BASED ON TRADITION

This brief overview of historical Belgian beers reveals key points of the evolution of the beer styles which are prevalent today. First, although Pils-type low-temperature fermented beers today occupy over 75 percent of the market, they do not represent an indigenous brewing tradition. High-temperature fermentation is the way Belgian beer has been made for centuries. Ale fermentation results in a beer with a stronger taste than low-temperature fermentation, and when people think of Belgian beer they naturally think of "lots of taste." Another companion practice to ale fermentation is infusion mashing in wort production. The decoction mashing procedure used in brewing pilseners is imported from the German-speaking brewing areas of Bavaria and Bohemia.

Another long standing tradition of Belgian brewers is the separate fermentation of the first and second runnings from the mash vessel. The resultant simple and double beers date from the Middle Ages. This naming of a Double, or Dubbel is today still used in Trappist and Abbey beers. Although the barley malt is the foundation of the mashing process, the addition of raw cereals such as wheat, barley, and oats has always been practiced in Belgium. The beer resulting from these blends is quite often unclear and appears flawed to the uninitiated. White beers are the new rage today and are a refined version of a brewing style that has been around for centuries. The blending of old beer with new beer is practiced nowhere else in the world that I know of. A beer with an acidic tang is often regarded today as a sign of poor quality control by large commercial brewers, yet brewers in certain areas of Flanders regard this as an example of their art. The Old Brown (*Veille Brune, Oud Bruin*) represents this technique. Herbs and spices which were the mainstay of the *gruitbeer* are today back in favor. White beers and some Specialty Beers make good use of traditional herbs and spices.

With such an array of traditional techniques, defining styles can be done only loosely. With the disappearance of trade barriers, competition is pan-European, requiring all of the modern brewer's skill and imagination. Within a few years old styles which are today dormant may be revived and modernized. The use of cereals other than malted barley is quite ancient. Although wheat is prevalent today it would not be a surprise to see a brewer come up with a new beer based on rye or oats. Who knows? Maybe in five years a combination of old ways with modern techniques could result in a beer style that is nonexistent today!

This is the way Belgians make beer: innovation based on tradition. Flemish brewers have up to now been more aggressive in this direction, but this is probably because their old tradition was more varied. Their more conventional counterpart in the French-speaking Walloon area have up to now been more conventional, but they are quickly catching up, especially the new generation of brewers.

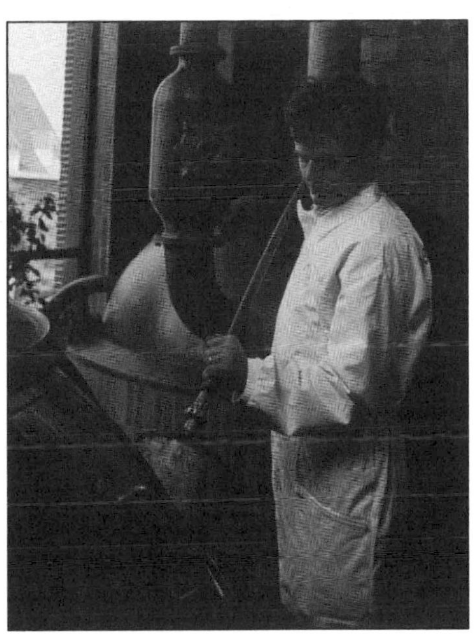

Brewing at Riva Brewery. Photo courtesy of Liefmans Brewery.

LEGAL CLASSIFICATIONS

When it comes to classifying Belgian beers into different categories, brewers have quite a bit of latitude. The legal requirements have nothing to do with styles. There are basically four legal classifications established. They apply only to original extract:

Category S (Superior) or Class S:	OG 1.062+ (15.5° Plato)
Category I or Class I:	1.044 to 1.054 (11 to 13.5° Plato)
Category II or Class II:	1.016 to 1.038 (4 to 9.5° Plato)
Category III or Class III:	up to 1.016 (up to 4° Plato)

Furthermore, the law allows the brewer to use up to 40

percent adjuncts in brewing. These can be in the form of raw grains such as wheat, corn, rice, barley, or they can be sugars. This classification is mainly useful for the tax collector, and is always written on the bottle label. For the consumers, it can imply alcoholic content to someone who is not quite familiar with a new brand.

The way a brewer operates in Belgium is quite different from the North American practice. A few days before brewing, the brewer must make a declaration of intention to brew to excise or revenue authorities in his locality. In this declaration he states that on such a date at such an hour he will brew a batch of a certain volume. He also states quantity of raw materials and their weight, along with the volume of water. Payment of excise tax is due upon submitting this declaration. On brewing day, the brewer will often have a visit from his local excise officer. The excise officer measures the volume of wort in the brew kettle and records the original specific gravity. Of course, he makes the appropriate corrections for differences caused by the temperature variations.

To measure these differences, he uses a legal hydrometer which is calibrated in Belgian legal degrees. This is why on certain Belgian bottles you see such fantastically high numbers as 12 degrees. These are in Belgian legal degrees and have nothing to do with the alcoholic content of the beer. There is a correspondence between these degrees and Plato degrees. The excise officer knows the correspondence of specific gravity to the declared raw materials. His job is to make sure that the wort corresponds to what is declared. This system of taxation has led to an interesting brewing method. Because tax is paid on the wort in the brew kettle, the brewer does everything possible to retain as much wort as possible. This has led to the practice of centrifuging the wort to clear it of the hot break. Some brewers even centrifuge the cooled wort. Spent hops are usually pressed to recover wort. After the main fermentation is over, the yeast is centrifuged and the recovered beer is added back, usually to the primary fermenter.

This classification system allows no beers to be brewed with an original extract of between 1.054 to 1.063 (13.5 to 15.5° Plato) or with specific gravity between 1.038 to 1.044 (9.5 to 11° Plato). This is important in classifying Belgian beer.

To better understand this requirement, a few words of explanation are necessary. A word quite commonly used in professional brewing textbooks is "attenuation." This word is used to express the difference between the original specific gravity or original extract of the wort prior to fermentation, and the final specific gravity after fermentation. It is usually expressed in a percentage basis.

Attenuation is calculated easily using the formula:

$$\frac{(E - E') \times 100}{E}$$

E is the original gravity in Plato degrees; E′ is the final gravity in Plato degrees.

For example, a wort of 12 degrees Plato (1.048) fermented down to 3 degrees Plato (1.012). Using the formula we obtain: (12 – 3) /12 x 100 = 75%.

In reality, taking the final gravity after fermentation does not truly represent the remaining extract. The final gravity reading is a combination of the remaining sugar in solution along with the alcohol that is now present. This is why brewers refer to this type of attenuation as apparent attenuation. In order to obtain the real attenuation we have to separate the alcohol from the beer, usually by distillation, and then measure the remaining extract. You can also consult tables that will list both the real attenuation and the alcohol content of a beer, given the apparent attenuation. Thus our example beer has a real attenuation of 60.8 percent resulting in an alcohol content of 4.8 percent v/v (volume per volume) or 3.75 v/w (volume per weight).

Returning to the classification of beer in Belgium we can deduce the following: You seldom encounter Belgian beers with an alcohol content in the range of between 6 percent to 7 percent v/v (4.7 percent to 5.5 percent v/w). If you do, it is probably a beer of 15.5° Plato extract not fully attenuated. How the brewer decides to classify his beer in terms of style is up to him, as long as it falls within legal requirements.

[(Beers in Category I have a maximum original extract of 13.5° Plato (1.054). Its apparent attenuation is 83 percent, and its real attenuation is 67.2 percent. The apparent residual extract is 2.3 (4.43 real), translating to 1.008 final gravity (2° Plato). This corresponds to an alcohol content of 6 percent v/v or 4.7 percent v/w. In Category S, the minimum extract is 15.5° Plato. Using the same attenuation criteria, the apparent attenuation is 83 percent (67.4 percent real attenuation), with an apparent residual extract of 2.6 (5.0 real residual extract), and a 1.010 final gravity (4° Plato). This corresponds to an alcohol content of 7 percent v/v or 5.47 v/w).]

In 1989, Belgium produced over 13 million hectoliters of beer. Of these, 2.4 million were exported. By beer type, this annual production is represented as:

Pils type beer : 74 % (9,750,000 hL)
Trappist beers: 2.2 % (286,000 hL)
Abbey beers: 1.9 % (250,000 hL)
Geuze or Lambic: 3.8% (500,000 hL)
Special Beer: 14% (1,800,000 hL)

Table beer: 3.8% (500,000 hL)
Alcohol free beer: 0.2 % (26,000 hL)

This book will deal mainly with beers from Categories S and I, classified as Trappist, Abbey, and Special. Although they represent only 18.1 percent of production, they account for 70 percent of non-Pils production and at least 400 of the 600-plus brand names in Belgium.

With these guidelines in mind, let's look at a way of defining Belgian beer that is more useful to the consumer and beer taster. When beer amateurs think of Belgian beer the first thing that comes to mind is Trappist beer. Let's take a better look at those beers.

2

Character Profiles of Belgian Beers

TRAPPIST AND ABBEY BEERS

People often wonder why monks brew beer. After all, monks are supposed to lead a life of prayer, away from worldly temptation. Why should they make a product which, according to some misguided souls, is a product of the devil — a worldly temptation which leads one to hell. A historical look at monastic life is appropriate in order to better understand this facet of brewing.

It seems that there have always been monks of one sort or another. Some of the prophets of the Old Testament led a reclusive life. Buddhist monks predate the Christian era. Up to the fourth century B.C., monks were simple individuals who led a life away from others. Some lived in the desert or other barren places. In the fourth century an Egyptian-born monk known as Pacome is credited with laying the foundation of organized communal life. The monastery of Tabennsi consisted of a walled compound with about 20 houses and a church. It also had a garden, a cellar and spare rooms for visitors and travelers. In France at Ligugé, south of Poitiers, a monastery was founded in 360 A.D. that still exists today.

When the patron saint of Ireland, St. Patrick, set out on his mission to the Emerald Isle in the early fifth century, he departed from a monastery on a Mediterranean island.

At that time, most of the monasteries were situated in southern Europe, and it was natural for the monks to grow grapes in their garden for wine. Later, when monks set out from Ireland to preach in the area that is today Germany, Belgium and Switzerland, it was natural for them to take up beer brewing. After all, the people living there were already brewers. Water was a beverage of doubtful quality and propagated many diseases. Beer, which consists primarily of water, was regarded as a safe beverage because the water used in brewing is boiled.

In the sixth century, the Italian monk St. Benedict, the founder of the famous monastery of Monte Cassino, is credited with laying down the rules of monastic life. He declared that each monastery would have a leader, the abbott, to whom monks would vow obedience. He ruled that monks would spend part of the day praying and part of the day working and he defined the schedule. He also mentioned that monasteries should be constructed in such a way as to have included in their walls everything necessary for their life: water, a garden, shop, etc. This way, monks would not have to go outside and face temptation.

In each monastery, the *cellerier,* a monk chosen for his good sense of administration, was made responsible for all the material things in the community. Dom Perignon, the inventor of Champagne, is the most famous *cellerier.* An additional duty of the *cellerier* was to take care of travelers. In those days monasteries were the logical place to stop. Hotels were few and far between, if they existed at all.

Throughout the Middle Ages monastic life flourished in Europe. Depending on the benevolence of the local lord, monasteries took different characters. Some were plain, religious places while others came to be known as centers of knowledge and learning. As with all good things there were abuses, and accordingly a need for reform. St. Bernard (circa 1090 to 1153) is recognized today as the father of the Cistercian order. He introduced a stricter version of the rules of St. Benedict, with an insistence on manual labor. At that time some monasteries owned vast properties and had major income from renting their lands to local peasants. The monks themselves actually did very little manual labour.

In the following centuries the Cistercian monastic life flourished in Europe, with over 500 monasteries. In the 17th century, a monk called Rancé established himself at the "Abbaye de la Trappe" in Normandy. He observed very strict monastic life and soon had many followers. They became known as the "Cistercians of strict observance," or as Trappist monks. Soon other Trappist monasteries were started in northern France and the surrounding area.

To ensure their livelihood, these monks made various products. Most of them were for their own use. Some were sold to the public, such as cheese and religious objects. But one activity was common to all of them: they all brewed beer, for their own use and for sale.

Some lords were very anxious to give land for the establishments of religious orders. It was considered by many to be an investment in life after death, compensation for deviations from the righteous life on earth. Abbeys thus came into existence in such places as Leffe, Grimbergen, and Floreffe. Most of them had extensive land holdings and produced, among other crops, both wheat and barley. At times they had conflicts with commercial brewers because, growing their own, they had access to raw material at a better price. Because of their lower cost of operation they could also use more ingredients resulting in a higher-quality beer than that of private brewers.

This coexistence of monastic breweries and private breweries came to a sudden stop in 1796, during the French Revolution. At that time Belgium was under French rule. All religious monasteries were looted and either sold or destroyed. During the next 40 years monastic life vanished. Sometime around 1830 several abbeys were re-established, however, only on a limited scale. Vast land holdings were a thing of the past. Trappist abbeys of Westmalle and Westvleteren were revived around 1835 and soon took up brewing on a small scale with used equipment. Chimay was founded in 1850 and Rochefort in 1887. Orval, which had been founded in 1132, reappeared only in 1926 and the brewery in 1931. Following the rules of St. Benedict, all the brothers were required to perform manual labor. What better manual labor could you find than brewing, especially when you have very little land? Abbeys belonging to other religious orders were also revived. However, without a strict rule of manual labor, none of them took up brewing again.

During the 1930s all Trappist monasteries made beer. The product was available only at the monasteries. World War II interrupted their efforts. Only after the end of the war did brewing resume and become the serious operation we know it as today. Although monks had been brewers for centuries, it is only in the last 40 years that they have made their beer more commercially available.

After their shaky restart in the 1940s, the beers brewed by Trappist monks slowly acquired a reputation. These beers usually had a higher-than-normal alcoholic content, and were all bottle-conditioned. Other brewers were quick to see a good thing, and so-called "Trappist beers" started to proliferate in the 1950s. On February 28, 1962, the A.S.B.L. Abbaye Notre Dame d'Orval received an injunction from the Belgian Trade and Commerce tribunal in Ghent that can be summarized as follows: "Only beers brewed under the strict and absolute control of the monks of the Trappist of the Cistercian Order can be called Trappist beers." This judgement is important because it gave a legal status to a certain beer style, which is respected in most countries in the world. But how do we transpose a legal definition of a style into a practical definition of a style?

Most people think of Trappist beer as a very strong, dark amber beer with yeast sediment in the bottle. They might have tasted one — a few brave souls might have tasted a dozen. But did you know that in Belgium there are over 141 different beers that fit loosely in this category?

In an attempt to classify, let's look at four groupings of "Trappist" beer: the legally defined "Trappist" beer; the so-called abbey beer (Bière d'Abbaye, Abdij Bier); — and two substyles: the double (*dubbel*) and the Tripple (*Trippel*).

But when we look at the product and, better yet, taste it, how do we put profile guidelines on it? How do you classify a style whose legal criteria produce beers which vary in color from, light gold to apricot gold, tawny brown to garnet brown? Where do you set the alcoholic content guidelines on a style where the beers may vary from as low as 5.2 percent alc./vol. in Orval, to as high as 11.2 percent alc./vol. for the 12° Abt from Westvletteren? How should the hop flavor be defined when you compare the dry hopped aroma and bitterness of Orval to the faint hop nose of Rochefort?

There are only two characteristics common to all Trappist beers: they are all top-fermented and bottle-conditioned. Let us not forget that at any time the Trappist monks could come out with a beer that would have a profile similar to that of a pale ale, if they wished. Legally, that beer is still called a Trappist beer. Therefore your understanding of the style must take this possibility into account.

- Trappist Beer Profiles -

Original specific gravity: 1.050–1.095 (12.5°–24° Plato)
Apparent final gravity: 1.010–1.022 (2.5°–5.5° Plato)
Apparent degree of attenuation: 70–80%
Real degree of attenuation: 55–65%
Reducing sugar as maltose: 1–2.5%
Acidity (as lactic acid): 0.2%
pH: 3.9–4.3
Bitterness: 5–9 HBU per 5 gallons; 20–45 IBU
Color: 3.5°–20° L
Alcohol: 4.2–8.9% w/v; 5.2–11.2% v/v

According to the legal definition, only the beers brewed under the direct control of the brothers of the following monasteries have the right to be called Trappist beer:

Abbaye Notre Dame de Saint Sixte (Sint Sixtus Abdij) Westvleteren,
Abbaye Notre Dame d'Orval,
Abbaye Notre Dame de Scourmont, Les Forges Chimay,
Abbaye Notre Dame de Saint Remy, Rochefort
Abbaye Notre Dame du Sacre Coeur, Westmalle

As mentioned previously, the only thing that these beers have in common is the appellation "Trappist" plus the fact that they are all top-fermented and bottle-conditioned. Strictly speaking, the appellation of Trappist beer is more a designation of origin than a classification of style.

They all taste, smell, and look different. The monks that brew them are at the same time traditional and innovative. For instance, nobody else has ever dared to brew a beer with a unique taste profile like Orval. Nobody has ever dared to copy their unique bottle style either. When the monks at Westmalle first came out with their "Trippel" (Tripple) they

Illustration by Vicki Hopewell.

were the innovators. They now have over 40 imitators. The beers made by the monks of Westvletteren used to have no label on the bottle. Only the cap identified the beer. New laws now require labels. Chimay has become such a well-known name that most people think all other "Trappist" beers are similar to it. When it is winter and you want to sit down in the company of a good warming beer, what better choice than a Rochefort 10°?

Although the above parameters broadly define a style, further refinement can identify a substyle. First let's examine the product made by the Trappist monks' competitors —Abbey beer. Although an injunction made them stop using the name Trappist, these beers did not cease to exist. On the contrary, they increased and nowadays every existing monastery or monastery in ruin will probably have its name attached to a beer. For some monasteries, having their beer brewed by commercial brewers made quite good sense. After all, the initial cost of installing a brewery can be quite prohibitive. In addition, the loss of brewing knowledge in monasteries that were idle more than a century rendered the revival even more problematic. Turning to commercial brewers was a way for these monasteries to capitalize on their name and earn a decent revenue from royalties.

As a whole, Abbey beer tends to be similar in taste and aroma to Trappist beers. The comments that apply to Trappist can also apply to the Abbey and vice versa. A recent survey listed 86 different Abbey-style beers. Again, trying to delimit this style can be quite presumptuous. As far as Belgians are concerned, if the name has religious connotation it is an Abbey beer. Every brewer is trying to come up with a winner. If that means using spices or blending in old beer which may or may not have been subject to bacterial or wild yeast modifications, it's fair game.

- Abbey Beer (Biere d'Abbaye, Abdij Bier) Profile -

Original specific gravity: 1.050–1.095 (12.5°–24° Plato)
Apparent final gravity: 1.010–1.022 (2.5°–5.5° Plato)
Apparent degree of attenuation: 70–80%
Real degree of attenuation: 55–65%
Reducing sugar as maltose: 1–2.5%
Acidity (as lactic acid): 0.2%
pH: 3.9–4.3
Bitterness: 5–9 HBU per 5 gallons; 20–35 IBU
Color: 3.5°–20° L
Alcohol: 4.2–8.9% w/v; 5.2–10% v/v

These guidelines are quite generous and give a general outline of what Abbey beers are like. If we look at the majority of beers with similarities in this style and not at the complete list, we can get a better idea of an Abbey-style beer. As far as flavor goes, the majority of them give a soft, malty fullness in the front of the mouth, a rather neutral taste, and an aftertaste on the sweet side. The hop flavor is very subdued. The majority of them are highly carbonated and the tingling sensation of carbon dioxide gives them a drier finish than the flavor warrants. Some also exhibit a bitter finish that is more a contribution of the yeast than the hops. The unique aftertaste of Abbey beers represents the particular signature of the yeast or yeasts used.

Aroma of Abbey beers is almost always fruity and estery due to top-fermentation. Most are subjected to a very high temperature in primary fermentation. It is not uncommon for the wort to reach 85 degrees F (30 degrees C) during the first or second day of the primary fermentation. The aroma is what the Belgians call sweet. This is particularly noticeable in beers that have had an addition of *candi* sugar in the kettle. Hop aroma is almost nonexistent, and the same applies to aromas developed by specialty grains. Here again, the yeast or yeasts employed contribute a certain uniqueness to each brand. The hops used are typically highly aromatic European varieties, used in small quantities. They blend with the other flavor components, contributing to the final taste while not being apparent.

However, some Abbey beers do not have the flavor and aroma pattern described above. A few have a profile similar to a strong pale ale, such as a Cuvée de l Ermitage. Some have a generous contribution of spice in their aromas, like the Corsendonk Agnus or the St. Benoît. These can be classified as Special as well as Abbey if the brewers so choose. A few have aromas that are more similar to a Lambic or an Oud Bruin, such as St. Idesbald. We will not elaborate on them here. The section ahead on Special Beers gives more details.

In the categories of Trappist and Abbey are two subclassifications that are more specific in style than the general profile given above. They are categorized as Double *(Dubbel)* and Tripple *(Trippel)* according to their alcoholic strength.

- Double *(Dubbel)* -

Original specific gravity: 1.063–1.070 (15.7°–17.5° Plato)
Apparent final gravity: 1.012–1.018 (3°–4.5° Plato)
Apparent degree of attenuation: 70–80%
Real degree of attenuation: 55–65%
Reducing sugar (as maltose): 1–2.5%
Acidity (as lactic acid): 0.2%
pH: 4.1–4.3
Bitterness: 5–7 HBU per 5 gallons; 18–25 IBU
Color: 10–14 °L
Alcohol: 4.8–5.9% w/v; 6–7.5% v/v
Carbon Dioxide: 2–3.5 volume

As previously noted, Double *(Dubbel)* for the French dates from the Middle Ages and describes a beer having a starting gravity of between 1.050 (12.5° Plato) and 1.070 (17.5° Plato). This subcategory holds fairly true, although the range of original extract is now more restricted. A Double is in all cases a dark-amber, almost brown beer. It has a faint hop aroma, usually a generous malty nose with differences in aromas created by yeasts specific to each brewer. Most Doubles are bottle-conditioned but some of them are sterile filtered or pasteurized. Examples are the Grimbergen Double or the Leffe Brune. These are brewed by subsidiaries of major Belgian brewers.

This subcategory of Abbey or Trappist beer is quite standard from one brewery to another. These beers are never hoppy. They can have a generous body but some of them are thin. Their predominant characteristic is a sweet aroma and nutty taste. Their dark-amber color is obtained with dark *candi* sugar. If any dark specialty malt is used it is in such a small quantity that it doesn't contribute to the taste. The term Double or *Dubbel* is always in great evidence on the label and very few brewers will differ from the standard profile. This is one of the few instances where if they vary they will call it something else or just call it an Abbey beer, without naming it Double.

- Tripple *(Trippel)* -

Original specific gravity: 1.070–1.095 (17.5°–24° Plato)
Apparent final gravity: 1.018–1.024 (4.5°–6.0° Plato)
Apparent degree of attenuation: 70–80%
Real degree of attenuation: 55–65%
Reducing sugar (as maltose): 1–2.5%
Acidity (as lactic acid): 0.2%
pH: 4.1–4.3

Bitterness: 5–7 HBU per gallons; 20–25 IBU
Color: 3.5–5.5°L
Alcohol: 5.6–8% w/v; 7–10% v/v

As with Doubles, the same kind of analysis can be used in the case of the Tripple. The classification Tripple is unknown in North America and is regarded by the Belgian beer drinker as a style in itself. It is the Belgian brewing style that is the easiest to classify. The style originated at the Trappist abbey of Westmalle. It is pale in color, usually made with only pale, Pils-type malt and a judicious addition (up to about 25 percent of total extract) of either glucose or *candi* sugar in the brew kettle. Its alcoholic strength will vary between 7 to 10 percent v/v. A recent survey listed 41 different brand names of Tripples on the market. These beers have a light, malty nose that can at times be neutral or have a faint aroma of hops. The best examples of the style have a very subtle alcohol undertone while others have a more predominant alcoholic taste, although that taste has a tendency to blend with aging. They are all bottle-conditioned.

There are two schools of thought regarding the origin of the style. Some, like myself, are of the opinion that a Tripple represents a beer with three times the extract value of what historically was known as the simple. The simple had a starting gravity of around 1.030 to 1.035 (7.5 to 8.8° Plato), the double has 1.060 to 1.070 (15 to 17.5° Plato) and logically a beer that has a starting gravity of 1.070 to 1.095 (17.5 to 24° Plato) should be called a Tripple. This fits the age-old brewing tradition.

The other school of thought says a Tripple is so named because it has had three fermentations. The first one is the primary fermentation, the second is secondary fermentation or aging, and, finally, the third is bottle-conditioning.

Although this is true, it is also true of many other beers. Lots of Doubles have also had the same three fermentations and most of the Specialty beers also have had it. Three fermentations is not unique, but having three times the extract of the simple is unique to Tripples.

Although the first example of this style was of Trappist origin (the Westmalle Trippel), the name soon began to be used by other brewers of abbey beers. But it was always applied to a beer that was a close replica of the Westmalle product. Nowadays the name Tripple or *Trippel* is quite often applied to a beer that has no monastic connections but is simply in the style originated by the monks of Westmalle.

Tripples are always similar to each other. Visually they are just a shade darker than a Pils. Their aroma can be neutral to malty or sweet. The hop aroma, if present, will be very subdued. Having a high volume of dissolved carbon dioxide, they always present a generous collar. In most cases the taste is quite neutral. The better examples have a generous mouthfeel. They are quite sweet in the finish. A few have a bitter aftertaste caused by the yeast used. The best examples have no alcoholic taste, they provide only a sensation of warmth. These are the most refreshing of the high-alcohol beers, which probably accounts for their increasing popularity.

In summary, Belgian Abbey-type ales fall into the following classes:

Trappist beers: Beers brewed directly under the supervision of Trappist monks. A legal classification. Only five such breweries exist.

Abbey beer: Beers brewed by commercial breweries, usually for an existing monastery. Others in this category have no monastic connections, they just use a religious-sounding name.

Double (*Dubbel*): A dark-amber Abbey or Trappist beer, 6 to 7.5 percent alcohol v/v. If, on a rare occasion, the name is used for a beer such as the Double Enghien which is not an Abbey or Trappist, it is not necessarily a dark-amber beer.

Tripple (*Trippel*): A straw-color, high-gravity brew from 7 to 10 percent alcohol v/v. A few of these are Abbey or Trappist but most are not. Although this style is of Trappist origin it should really be in a class by itself.

SPECIAL BEERS

How do we classify all beers with an alcohol content of above 7 percent v/v or below 6 percent v/v that do not fit in the usual categories? Hypothetically, if a brewer already makes an abbey style beer of 8 percent v/v and he wishes to brew another similar one but a different color or taste how does he classify it? Easy! He just gives it a name such as Lucifer, Duvel, Piraat, Delirium Tremens, MacChouffe, or Gulden Draak and classifies it as a *Bière Spéciale* (Special Beer). What about a beer that has an alcohol content of 6 percent, brewed with a gourmet assortment of herbs and spices? Here again, just call it a Special Beer. There are even brewers who ferment and bottle their beer with one yeast and call it an abbey style beer, then bottle the same beer with a different yeast or a different priming sugar, give it another name and call it a Special. As long as they are within the range of the legal requirements, anything goes.

Although some brewers use the easy route in fabricating their Special beers, others truly put an effort into creating an individual product. The Artevelde Grand Cru from the Huyghe brewery in Melle is a good example of a Special Beer at 5.6 percent v/v with a distinctive, woodsy taste resulting from the use of two yeasts. The Gouden Carolus from Het Anker in Mechelen is another unique-tasting product, combining the aroma of old beer with grape and fig undertones. Duvel, from the Moortgat brewery in Breedonk, is probably the most successful of the Specials on the Belgian market.

In this category you will usually encounter hoppy beers. However, what the Belgians call a hoppy beer is not quite the same as what North Americans call a hoppy beer. To Belgians, hoppiness is more subtle and more refined. Traditional American aromatic hops such as Cascade are unknown. Belgian brewers use generous amounts of low-bitterness European varieties such as Saaz, Hallertauer or Styrian. This gives a generous hoppy and spicy aroma without the accompanying bitterness.

- Category S Profile -

Original specific gravity: 1.063–1.095 (15.5°–24° Plato)
Apparent final gravity: 1.012–1.022 (3°–5.5° Plato)
Apparent degree of attenuation: 70–80%
Real degree of attenuation: 55–65%
Reducing sugars (as maltose): 1–2.5%
Acidity (as lactic acid): 0.2%
pH: 3.9–4.3
Bitterness: 5–9 HBU per 5 gallons; 20–50 IBU
Color: 3.5–20 °L
Alcohol: 5.5–9.6% w/v; 7–12% v/v
Carbon Dioxide: 1.5 to 3.5 vol.

From the above guidelines we can see that there is a great deal of latitude in brewing beer in this category. A recent survey of this category listed 76 different brand names. Most of the beers are quite different, but they have a few things in common. The majority of them are bottle-conditioned. Of those that are filtered quite a few are pasteurized. Even some of the bottle-conditioned ones are pasteurized. Their carbon dioxide content is usually quite high. Most Belgian brewers are high primers. It is not uncommon to have foam gush out of the bottle. This is the category where one finds the most beers with aromas and tastes due to spices. Although coriander and orange peel are quite common, brewers also use small quantities of ginger, cumin, paradise or cardamom seeds, and nutmeg to achieve unique taste and flavor profiles. One brewer is even reported to use a small portion of basil. Another has a beer named Minty's that has the aroma of mint. Each brewer has his own trade secret and each is looking for something different to catch the public's fancy.

Although generally speaking Belgian beers are not hoppy, this category is certainly the hoppiest. Off all the Belgian brewers surveyed, only the Trappist brewery of Notre Dame d'Orval uses dry hopping. The others impart their hop aroma in the brew kettle. The advent of hop oils extracted with carbon dioxide might change the picture. It is reported that these extracts can be conveniently used to enhance the hop aroma. Brewers who brew specials should refrain from using varieties such as Cascade. High-alpha-acid hops should also be used with caution. Most of the Belgian brewers look on them with suspicion, preferring to use noble varieties even for bittering. They are said to produce a rounder bitterness that is more pleasant.

Although Belgian beer drinkers are quite fond of stouts such as Guinness, Whitbread Extra Stout, Mackeson Stout, and Bass Stout, they do not brew them on a large scale. The ones generally available are either brewed in England or brewed in Belgium under licence. The public regards this as a British specialty and looks for the British product. This is why in the Special beer category you do not find beers that contain significant amounts of roasted or black malts. The darker ones are usually made with a slight amount of crystal malt but most of the color is obtained by using brown candi sugar. The great majority of the beers in this category use candi, either white or brown, to attain their high level of original extract. Some brewers also use glucose in combination with candi, especially in lighter-colored beers.

Some brewers specializing in this category (one of them produces over 30 different brands) use different yeasts in a common wort to obtain specific taste profiles. In this way different attenuations, with corresponding alcohol levels, can be obtained. Special yeasts can also be added in the secondary fermentation or even at bottling to achieve the desired effect. Some even have the acidic aroma and flavor one would expect in an Oud Bruin (see description). Usually this is obtained with the help of a wild-type yeast, either in the primary or the secondary fermentation. The St. Idesbald is typical of beer using this process. Although present in the bottle, these yeasts are usually slow-acting and are not usually used as priming yeast.

- Category I Profile -

Original specific gravity: 1.044–1.054 (11°–13.5° Plato)
Apparent final gravity: 1.006–1.012 (1.5°–3° Plato)
Apparent degree of attenuation: 77–86%
Real degree of attenuation: 62–70%
Reducing sugars (as maltose): 1–2.5%
Acidity (as lactic acid): 0.2%
pH: 3.9–4.3
Bitterness: 5–9 HBU per 5 gallons; 20–35 IBU
Color: 3.5–20 °L
Alcohol: 3.2–4.8% w/v; 4–6% v/v
Carbon Dioxide: 1.5 to 3.5 vol.

There are fewer beers in this category than in the Category S. The beers in this category are in direct competition with Pils, ales, and the white beers. Their taste and aroma profile is essentially the same as an ale with the following exceptions: a) They often have higher hop levels, b) Some of them can be quite bitter, like La Gaumaise by Maire, c) Spices can also be more assertive here than in Saisons, (see description), d) No particular brand in this category has achieved notoriety, e) Most brewers have concentrated their efforts in the higher-alcohol, higher-profit varieties.

ALES & SAISONS

Traditionally, Belgian brewers have always been top-fermenters. Although the popularity of regular strength top-fermented beer has declined since the turn of the century, it still enjoys a very sizeable portion of devotees. When bottom fermentation became popular, over a century ago, it was for one principal reason: Beer fermented at cold temperatures was, on average, better than beer fermented at warmer temperatures and, if kept cold, maintains stability longer. Additionally, the use of ice made brewing possible nearly throughout the year.

In contrast, top-fermented beers were more subject to variations caused by high fermenting temperatures. Ale brewing was basically a winter activity. Breweries were closed during the hot summer months of June, July, and August. Production resumed in September. This schedule was a necessity for cooling the wort.

Hot wort was usually left over night in big shallow basins known as coolships. A few years ago during a visit to one of the major brewers in Belgium, the Maes brewery, I saw two coolships that were still in use. One was copper and the other was made out of stainless steel. According to the brewer, they were still the best tools available for producing a bright, trub-free wort. At a depth of no more than 6 inches (15 cm), the wort decants quickly, resulting in clear wort, but in contacting the surrounding air it also acquires various microorganisms. In the winter this is less of a problem (first, because the wort cools even more quickly and secondly, there are less active and viable microorganisms in the air). The beer also ferments at a slower rate. Historically, brewers knew that beer made in the winter was of better quality than beer made at any other time.

Fermentation techniques were also quite different from today. When the wort cooled to fermentation temperature, the beer from the coolship was transferred and divided among numerous small individual tanks known as *cuves guilloires*. Then the yeast collected from a good previous fermentation was added. As soon as signs of fermentation appeared—sometimes within a few hours, sometimes overnight—the young fermenting wort was transferred to individual casks of an even smaller capacity. Left behind in the *cuve guilloires* were all the dead yeast cells and trub deposits. A few hours after the casks had been filled, yeast would escape through the bung hole, which was left open. The overflowing yeast was collected when fermentation was most active and used for pitching new batches.

Needless to say this fermentation method left the door open for all kinds of activities by neighboring microorganisms. Fermentation usually lasted two to three days. The brewer in charge of the fermentation would add fresh wort at regular intervals to replace the beer that had been lost with the outgoing yeast. He knew that as long as thick, yellowish yeast foam came through the bung, fermentation was not finished. But as soon as the foam turned white, he knew it was over. The white foam came slowly out through the bung hole, looking like a cauliflower. This was known as the cauliflower stage and it was then that the brewer added isinglass to help in clarifying the beer and close the bung. This was known as *collage* which, roughly translated, means "gluing." Glue was commonly made from fish and water. To the brewer, this mixture of fish swim bladders and water was just another form of glue (colle). The beer was left bunged up for a few days to acquire natural carbonation and thereafter was quickly delivered to the local outlets to be served directly from the casks.

Successful ale brewers at the time usually concentrated on a very local market. Beer was fermented quickly, delivered locally, and drunk quickly. It is easy to deduce how this beer tasted. It had a pronounced yeasty taste, was probably a bit cloudy and was served with a low carbonation level. In contrast, beer fermented with a bottom-fermenting yeast at a cold temperature and aged for a while was less yeasty, quite clear, and had a higher carbonation level. This Pilsener-type beer, with its smoother and mellower taste soon acquired new devotees. They were quite often people that had never liked beer before because of the rough ale taste, although many ale drinkers also switched over.

But ale kept a loyal following. The bottom-fermented Pilseners were usually premium beers, with an alcohol content of around 5 percent v/v and because their fermentation and aging took longer, the brewer accordingly charged a bit more. Ale allowed the brewer to have a faster turnover and thus be more competitive in price. Most of the beer at that time was sold on draft in taverns. The beer drinkers were mostly laborers engaged in low-paying work, so prices needed to be low. Quite a few low-gravity beers were available at that time. They were made from the second runnings of the mash tank. Again, this gave the ale brewer a price advantage, and the consumer a volume advantage.

A brewery official once remarked to me during a visit

that when it comes to the regular strength beer, Pils or ale, you really are facing two different markets. On the one hand you have the Pils drinker who is basically a one-brand man. He likes his Pils, his brand, and he does not switch around easily. He hardly tries anything else. He will probably never try an ale. He is the typical beer drinker found throughout the world. On the other hand, the ale drinker is a more discriminate drinker. He is more likely to try something different than the Pils drinker. Although less numerous, ale drinkers are at times in higher concentrations in cities, and when they are, ale becomes the most prevalent style of the region. This explains why, in a large city such as Antwerp, the popular local beer is De Koninck, an ale. And rightly so, when one realizes that ale has been the style of Antwerp for centuries. A century ago all the brewers in the region were top-fermenters.

Equally true is the situation in the French-speaking Walloon region. The regions of Mons, Charleroi, and Namur are situated over an immense coal area. Coal attracted heavy industry and workers with big thirsts to satisfy. Here again, top-fermented beers were in favor.

Because of Pasteur's pioneer work in microbiology between 1860 and 1870, brewers soon began to understand the process better. Soon the same microbiological controls used in low-temperature fermentation became the norm for ale brewers, with the exception that ale fermentation took place at a higher temperature. The resulting ale acquired more finesse.

Earlier I mentioned beer made from the second runnings. But what about the first running? What did the brewers do with it? The infusion mashing method that obtained two different worts was usually reserved for winter. Although the fermentation methods before the twentieth century left much to be desired, brewers knew that beer fermented from wort made in the dead of winter kept better. Therefore, why not make a special beer? So they brewed beers in winter to be drunk in the summer season. This is how Saison came about. Quick cooling of the wort, coupled with an active, quick fermentation resulted in a cleaner-tasting beer. A long, cold storage period gave the ale a smooth, mellow finish with a definite ale taste.

Today ales remain very popular in Belgium. The most popular brands are brewed by medium-sized brewers. Examples are Special Palm by Palm, and De Koninck by De Koninck in Antwerp. Even the biggest brewer in Belgium, the Interbrew group, proudly advertises its Vieux Temps as a traditional Belgian-style beer. (Vieux Temps is made by Interbrew's subsidiary, the Mont St. Guibert Brewery.)

- Ale and Saison Profile -

Original specific gravity: 1.044–1.054 (11°–13.5° Plato)
Apparent final gravity: 1.006–1.012 (1.5°–3° Plato)
Apparent degree of attenuation: 79–85%
Real degree of attenuation: 64–70%
Reducing sugars (as maltose): 1–2.5%
Acidity (as lactic acid): 0.2%
pH: 3.9–4.3
Bitterness: 5–8 HBU per 5 gallons; 20–30 IBU
Color: 3.5–12° L
Alcohol: 3.2–4.8% w/v; 4–6% v/v
Carbon Dioxide: 1.5 to 3.5 vol.

These beers are available on draught, usually in the region of the brewery. Elsewhere they are more often found in bottles. They have similarity to British pale ales and are often called pale ale. The main difference is that they are not as hoppy. A British drinker would probably find them more similar to keg beer than a bitter. Another major difference is in their extract content. The majority of the British beers on the market have an initial gravity of 1.040 (10° Plato) whereas Belgian ales have an initial gravity of 1.048 (12° Plato). As a result, Belgian ales are fuller tasting than their British counterparts. But their higher carbonation level creates an equilibrium between the mellow, malty taste and the lower level of hoppiness. Most of the beers in this category have been filtered but some are bottle conditioned with a resulting yeast deposit. Filtered beers are quite stable in taste but bottle-conditioned ones are subject to what is known as taste evolution. In other words, a young sample might taste totally different from a more mature sample. A good example of this phenomenon is the Saison Regal. Freshly bottled samples have an obvious coriander aroma that completely disappears in two months.

The first quality one notices when presented with a glass of ale is the inviting, creamy foam collar that seems to keep all the aroma from escaping the glass. It is the practice in Belgium to serve every beer in a special glass designed specifically for its style, and ales are no exception. For example, De Koninck serves its ale in a chalice-type glass suggesting more of a religious ceremony than just a glass of beer. The full, fruity aroma that emanates from the glass fills your nose. The malt is evident but the hops are subdued. They are there but more to underline than assert, and usually they are of the finest type, either from Czechoslovakia or Bavaria. Diacetyl is not present.

Saisons sometimes have a hint of acidity in the nose. The difference in aroma between each beer is primarily caused by the different strain of yeast used. Some brewers use the same yeast in the fermentation of a high-gravity beer and a normal-gravity beer. The two beers can have totally different aroma patterns. Usually the yeast has a more individual signature at low gravity than at high gravity.

The first sip of an ale or Saison fills your mouth instantly with a mellow, fruity, smoothness. The front of the mouth first detects the presence of sweetness from the malt. A fairly high carbonation level causes a prickly effect in the mouth, but soon disappears to be replaced by a long lasting dryish aftertaste. Here again, hop flavor is present but not assertive. The bitterness level is very subdued, and if at all present, is caused more by the particular yeast employed. At times Saisons develop a lightly acidic secondary aftertaste, mostly encountered in older samples.

Because beers in this category do not have high alcohol content, one should not expect to feel the warming effect of alcohol. As a rule, these beers are brewed with either pale Pils malt or, less often, ale malt. Specialty grains such as crystal malt can be employed, but not highly roasted grains. Quite often, deeper colors are obtained by adding a small quantity of dark *candi* sugar in the kettle. Soft water is used for brewing. Because of the low level of hoppiness in these beers, hard water would undoubtedly result in a lingering, bitter mineral taste.

WHITE BEER (BIERE BLANCHE, WIT BIER)

Throughout Belgian brewing history there is mention of beer brewed with a generous proportion of wheat. This wheat was always in an unmalted form, so it can only be assumed that the resulting beers were cloudy. It is generally conceded that the most popular and successful wheat beer of bygone days was brewed in the town of Leuven (Louvain). This industrial city, situated a few kilometers from Brussels, is today in the Flemish part of Belgium. It is the seat of one of the oldest Universities in Europe. Founded in 1425, the

Katholieke Universiteit van Leuven (L'Université Catholique de Louvain) has acquired a solid reputation not only as an intellectual center but also as a brewing school. One of the most respected brewing researchers of this century, Jean De Clerck, was the director of its brewing school for years, and a lot of knowledge taken for granted today is the result of his pioneering work.

However, only a few centuries ago, brewing was not as much a scientific activity as it was a process of trial and error. This was especially true for brewing processes using raw wheat, an ingredient that is notoriously difficult to utilize. This is because wheat has a gelatinization temperature range of between 125.5 to 147 degrees F (52 to 64 degrees C). Although the degradation of the cell walls that make it suitable for conversion by the malt enzyme takes place at the proper temperature, the result is a viscous solution that is difficult to filter through the mash vessel. Brewers came up with very ingenious mashing methods to circumvent these difficulties.

One tool that was quite commonly used at the turn of the century was the *stuykmanden*. This was basically a big basket made of wicker or, in later times, copper. These baskets were lowered onto the surface of the mash through the top of the mash tank, where they acted as strainers and allowed the liquid portion of the mash to filter through. When the *stuykmanden* was filled the contents were siphoned into a holding tank or brew kettle. This permitted otherwise viscous solutions to be moved from one vessel to the other, something that would have been impossible by filtering through the false bottom of the mash tun. The use of the *stuykmanden* was of absolute necessity in brewing wheat beers.

The whole mashing procedure was quite complex and, although the resulting beer was good, the time and equipment required probably had a good bit to do with the demise of its popularity. The brewing process required four vessels: two brew kettles, a mash or clarification tank, and a holding tank.

Two different mixtures of grains were prepared. The first one, which consisted of 60 percent of the total, had 46 parts malted barley, eight parts raw oats, and six parts raw wheat. This was known as the *goed sakken* and was coarsely ground. The remaining 40 percent was called the *vet sakken* and consisted of four parts malted barley and 36 parts raw wheat. The *vet sakken* was always a finer grind than the *goed sakken*.

Brewing began by filling the mash tank with cold water. The *goed sakken* was added and a group of brewers mixed it until thoroughly hydrated. In those days the mixing was always done by men with long handed spoons known as *fourquet*. They would let the mash rest for a few minutes and then they would lower the *stuykmanden* and draw off the liquid portion. This was white with raw starch and, as the first wort, was directed to brew kettle number I. In the meantime, brew kettle number II, which had been previously filled with water, was fired up. As soon as all the liquid from this first mash had been drawn off, a second portion of warmed water from brew kettle number II was added to the mash tank. Again this was thoroughly mixed and drawn off through the *stuykmanden* to brew kettle number I. A third mash was prepared with water from brew kettle number II which by that time was boiling. After a rest, this third mash was drawn off through the top with the *stuykmanden* and toward the end through the false bottom. By then brew kettle number I was filled to 75 percent of its capacity and quickly fired up. As soon as it was filled, the second grain mixture (*vet sakken*) was added to the mash tank and thoroughly mixed. Whatever liquid portion was

An example of turn-of-the-century equipment is this mash tank, still used at the Crombe brewery. Made of steel, the whole gear-driven structure and paddles rotate continuously during the mashing process. Photo by Pierre Rajotte.

left from the third mash was directed toward a holding vessel.

While brew kettle number I was brought to a boil, the complete grain mixture in the mash tank went through a fourth, fifth and at times a sixth mash. These were all done with boiling water and a mash rest of 30 minutes each time. As soon as each mash was completed the wort was sent to the holding tank. When all the mashes were finished and brew kettle number II was empty, a portion of the contents of the holding tank was pumped back to fill kettle number II, which was immediately fired up. About a third was left behind in the holding tank. As soon as kettle number II reached the boiling point, hops were added. It was kept boiling for an hour and a half, and then the contents were pumped to the coolship. The hops were left behind in the brew kettle. They were used again for the boil of "small beer." The spent grains were not removed from the mash tank.

Until brew kettle number I reached the boiling point, its contents were thoroughly mixed by a group of brewers. Brew kettle number I was kept boiling with the vet sakken for at least an hour. Then the fire was shut down. As soon as the grain had settled, the *stuykmanden* was lowered. The boiling wort was drawn off and directed over the spent grain bed of the *goed sakken* left behind in the mash tank. It was held there for a while until it settled. As soon as kettle number I had been emptied of wort through the *stuykmanden* the rest of the wort in the holding tank was pumped in, mixed with the mash, and the kettle was fired up again.

The wort of the mash tank was recirculated through the holding tank until it was clear. As soon as it was clear it was pumped to the coolship. The second charge of brew kettle number I was handled the same way as the first charge. It was pumped to a coolship but was not mixed with the first one.

Sometimes a third mash using only water was done. The resulting "small beer" was handled the same way but kept apart from the main mash. This small beer was transferred to brew kettle number II which by now had been emptied of its wort. The small beer is brewed with the same hops that were used with the first boil. After the boil, it was transferred over to a coolship.

So there were four different worts cooling down in the coolships: one hopped, two unhopped, and the small beer which has been hopped with the spent hops of the first wort. As soon as they were cooled the worts were racked to the *cuve guilloire* where they were mixed before adding the yeast. The casks were topped with small beer if required. As soon as signs of fermentations were apparent, the contents were transferred to big wooden kegs where the primary fermentation took place. Fermentation continued in the ale tradition. The yeast was collected through the bung hole and the kegs were topped with fresh wort. Fermentation completed in four to five days. As soon as it slowed, the kegs were bunged up and immediately shipped. No finings are used, so the resulting beer had a milky, white appearance, from which it derived its name. The kegs were tapped and served quickly. "White Beer" had to be consumed in two to three weeks in the summer, but could be kept four to five weeks in winter. After that it became too acidic.

A portion of this beer was also bottled in small jugs. This was usually done when the beer was no more than one week old. It was claimed to be very sparkling and refreshing.

It is quite easy to gather from the above description why this brewing style has almost disappeared. The process was long and complicated, and the resulting beer was also very fragile, for obvious reasons. Unhopped wort left overnight to cool was a prime candidate for contamination. But this was probably desired. Bacteria acidified the wort. After these infected worts were mixed with hopped wort, bacteria was inhibited; and as soon as fermentation started and lowered the pH that was the end for the wort bacteria. During fermentation yeast was the lead actor, and bacteria was subdued to a supporting role. But once fermentation was over different kinds of lactic acid bacteria came into action. However, because the beer was consumed rapidly, they just imparted a pleasant tang that made the white beer famous as a refreshing summer beverage. Of course, if left too long in contact with the bacteria the effect became unpleasant, and the acidifying activity too great.

By the 1950s and 60s "white beer" had disappeared from Louvain. It came back to life in the 1970s in Hoegaarden, a small municipality a few miles from Louvain. Hoegaarden had also been famous for its white beer. Until a few years ago there were only two breweries making white beer in Belgium: Hoegaarden with the Hoegaarden Wit Bier, and Riva with the Dentergem Wit Bier. In 1990, however, you could find more than 20 different brand names. It seems that everybody is now making *wit bier.* Traditionally it was brewed only in the Leuven-Hoegaarden area but now it is produced everywhere in Belgium. The Moortgat and Palm breweries have united to market Steendonck. Huyghe in Melle brews Blanche des Neiges. De Gouden Boom is the proud maker of Blanche de Bruges, or Brugs Tarwebier as it is locally known. The big Walloon brewer Du Bocq even makes a Blanche de Namur in a region that is better known for Saison than *wit bier.* Its pleasant, tart, refreshing taste is appreciated in many circles and is a good export product for the Belgian brewers.

Of course nowadays nobody brews wheat beer like they did at the turn of the century. At that time wheat malt was almost unknown. Even today wheat is considered more difficult to malt than barley. Wheat has no husk and the germinating acrospire can be readily damaged. But modern equipment makes its malting possible on a large commercial scale. The use of wheat malt in the mash tank makes life much simpler for the brewer. The resulting wort is not as viscous and can be handled with the brewing vessels currently in use. The production process requires the same time needed for other kinds of beers. Knowledge of microbiology allows the brewer adequately to monitor his process to achieve a beer that has the same qualities as the product of bygone years but without the risk of surprises.

- White Beer *(Biere Blanche, Wit Bier)* Profile -

Original specific gravity: 1.048 (12° Plato)
Apparent final gravity: 1.008–1.010 (2°–2.5° Plato)
Apparent degree of attenuation: 78–83%

Real degree of attenuation: 63–68%
pH: 3.5–4.0
Bitterness: 5.5–7 HBU per 5 gallons; 15–25 IBU
Color: 2.5–4° L
Alcohol: 3.8–4.4% w/v; 4.8–5.2% v/v

If you prefer crystal clear beer, stop reading here and go to the next chapter. The main characteristic of a white beer is that it is white. This is probably the only beer style that has that characteristic. Of course it is not white like milk, but when seen through a bottle or a glass, the beer has a whitish veil. Another characteristic is its tart, faintly acidic, almost dry finish. A good pH value to aim for is 3.9. If the pH is lower, extra body is beneficial to balance the higher acidity. One brewer makes sure that his beer stays at 3.9 by pasteurizing it. I must add that I have tasted white beers with a pH of 3.5 that were extremely pleasant and refreshing. White beer is always a beer with high levels of carbon dioxide and, when poured, it quite often wants to jump out of the glass.

The aroma of current examples of white beer varies from brewery to brewery. Hop aroma has no business in white beer. Traditionally, aged hops were used so as not to impart aromas. The brewers wanted the preservative qualities of the hops, but not the aromatic qualities. The majority of white beers have a slight malty nose. This aroma reflects both the malted barley and the malted wheat. The clove aroma typical of Bavarian wheat beer is not found in Belgian white beer. This specific aroma is mostly the result of yeasts used in Bavaria. The yeasts used in Belgium do not give that clove aroma.

The aroma should reflect the generous amount of wheat used, although this can be sometimes hard to detect because of spices also used. In Belgian brewing circles, the use of spices is centuries old, and it is easy to imagine why.

Imagine coolships left overnight with unhopped wort. Although in winter this probably went without problems, it is easy to imagine that at times various bacterial visitors left their calling cards. Unable to detect a slightly altered wort, brewers must have had unpleasant surprises upon tapping a keg. What better way to mask unpleasant odors than spices? So it became more or less the norm to add a small quantity of spices—mostly coriander, and dried, bitter orange peel—either in the brew kettle or in the fermenting wort. Today minute quantities of other spices such as ginger and nutmeg are added by brewers who are trying to create their own unique aroma. Most white beers will have a pleasant, subdued aroma of spices. Spices can be added in any number of steps: in the brew kettle at knock out, in the whirlpool tank, with the priming solution at bottling, etc. Each brewer has his own method. One thing about spices is that after a while their aroma will vanish almost completely, blending with the beer's own aroma. Some brewers do not use spices and rely more on the aroma from their yeast. Wheat beer is truly a beer that has a changing taste. Its taste can vary enormously with time. But it is a beer that is meant to be drunk young.

Another major characteristic of white beer is its acidic aftertaste. In the old days the production process was enough to achieve this naturally. Nowadays brewers use various methods to acquire that special tang. Some ferment with a controlled level of lactic acid bacteria that are known to give an adequate acid taste without unpleasant side tastes. Others add lactic acid solutions at bottling. Others use lactic acid solutions to adjust to the right acidity level. Most of the bottled versions are bottle-conditioned. When the proper acid and carbonation level is reached, some even pasteurize the bottle-conditioned beer. Even without reverting to these processes, white beer will with time acquire a pleasant tartness. The process chosen is usually determined by how fast the brewer wants to sell the beer.

White beer is usually brewed by the infusion process. It can be done at a constant temperature or with increasing temperatures. Mashing in at low temperatures (below 121 degrees F or 50 degrees C) will in all cases acidify the wort. The resulting beer might differ in mouthfeel. Usually white beer fills your mouth with a well-rounded fullness that is overcome quickly by the tingle of carbonation. Soon a pleasant tartness spreads through the mouth, followed at times by a lingering and subdued acidic aftertaste. Hop bitterness is never predominant; it is always present but not noticeable. Here again, favored hops are the noble European varieties. In all cases the mouthfeel is full but never sweet, and the finish is always dry.

OUD BRUIN

The *Oud Bruin* or old brown style is regarded by various observers as either one of the most distinguished forms of the brewing art or a style of beer that should be banished. For the commercial brewer, who spends the major part of his day assuring himself that any piece of equipment that comes in contact with either the raw materials or the finished beer is scrupulously sanitized, working with wild yeasts and bacteria seems an odd way of making beer. But to the brewer who practices the art of crafting the *Oud Bruin* this represents an additional challenge. Not only must he concern himself with the regular problems of brewing, but he also must deal with bacteria and wild yeast with the same care that others practice to get rid of them. The bacteria and wild yeasts are as important in achieving the taste of this beer as is the regular yeast.

Another difference between commercial brewers and

Oud Bruin brewers is choice of equipment. Nowadays brewers would not even consider making beer in anything but stainless steel equipment, especially in North America. But we must remember that sophisticated stainless steel equipment is new to the brewing scene. Even after World War II it was still quite common, even in North America, to ferment and package in wooden vessels. In Europe, brewing has always been more regional than in North America. The village brewer is still a reality. Many of them, even in Germany, still use wooden fermenting vessels and casks with their associated risks.

The fear of beer going bad has always been the bane of the brewer. But what do we do with the bad beer? Dump it or sell it? Even today brewers face the same dilemma. This is why brewers guilds and corporations came into existence in the Middle Ages. They were instituted to protect the customers' interest and, of course, the brewers'. During that period there was no knowledge of microbiology and bad beer was quite often the result of low quality or insufficient quantity of ingredients. But the best brewers have always been the most conscientious and careful ones. Somewhere in history a good brewer probably tapped an old keg of beer that had been lying around or simply misplaced in a far corner. The less inquisitive person might have discarded it. But some curious soul tasted it. The taste was of old beer, with an aroma like sherry or port. It was probably acidic, most likely sour. The taste was probably good enough to have a second sip and maybe a third. Maybe he was curious enough to mix it with a newer beer. Then it probably tasted better. The next thing was to try it with a customer or client. Perhaps they liked it too. Suddenly the brewer was facing a new problem: how do I go about making more?

Suspecting that there was something good in that old keg he probably did not clean it. He just filled it up and let it age again. A few months later, a sampling revealed the same taste. It was sour, tangy, acidic but very pleasant. Now he had to increase production. At a certain stage he certainly mixed the contents of this magic keg into other kegs. The whole process surely took years to perfect, maybe centuries. One thing is certain, the brewers that practice the art of brewing sour beer today are the most traditional group encountered in Belgium. Generally they use antiquated equipment that they would never consider changing. Their method of operation and fermentation is similar to ones described in centuries-old brewing text books. And they have one thing in common: they are always secretive about their fermentation and aging practices.

Lactic acid bacteria such as *lactobacillus* and *pediococcus* have always been the bane of the commercial brewer. He is concerned with only one thing: getting rid of them. And he is right. They impart a harsh acidic taste to beer that is most unpleasant, especially when you brew a beer that is light in taste. But, as in any field of scientific activity, interested observers have looked upon bacteria with a different perspective. They are more concerned with the lifestyles of the bacteria, their likes and dislikes, their food requirements, etc. They have observed them so thoroughly that they have classified them into numerous categories. To the casual observer or even to a brewery microbiologist *lactobacillus* is an enemy to be conquered and destroyed. If they were to look at them more closely they might find that, although it gives an acidic taste, that its taste is not all that unpleasant. This is what the *Oud Bruin* brewers did before microbiology even existed. They also discovered what science would later demonstrate: bacteria is very sensitive to environment. Any slight change can prevent growth.

It is a well-known fact among brewery microbiologists that culturing a lactic acid bacteria found in your beer is quite difficult to do. Some of the strains are almost impossible to culture. The *Oud Bruin* brewers have been able to perpetuate the environment of their good bacteria because they are such traditionalists. Most of them still use wooden casks for secondary fermentation. These casks are cleaned now and then—"rinsed" is probably the more appropriate word. A lot of the success of brewing sour beer lies in good blending.

Primary fermentation is usually accomplished in an open fermenter. At this stage the brewer likes to utilize a healthy yeast that is as clean as possible. During secondary fermentation, he can start to exercise options. He can age his beer for over a year as a clean beer. This way he will obtain a beer that will acquire an old vinous taste but not necessarily a sour taste. The aroma and taste of the beer will be like port or sherry. He can also age it in selected casks which are known to promote pleasant sour and acidic tastes. He also has the option to age his beer for only a short while, which again will result in a beer with a different taste profile. Various wild yeasts are also known to give vinous, acidic aromas. Some brewers use these in secondary fermentation to achieve various taste profiles. Brewers desiring to dabble in these yeasts should be cautious. They are usually slow starters and if present in a main fermentation could actually retard it. Most of them are usually of a powdery nature and settle very slowly. Long aging is required in order to achieve clarity.

Competence at the blending stage is only acquired by experience. Long years of trial and error and trading information by word-of-mouth are the reasons why these craft brewers are reluctant to divulge too much of their technique.

The continuing success of this beer style has prompted some brewers to accelerate the process. Nowadays it is possible to culture various strains of these friendly lactic acid bacteria on a commercial basis. Enterprising brewers are now able to fabricate various blends of sour beers by using these commercial cultures. The accelerated process reduces the need for wooden casks and storage room. These beers are usually filtered before bottling. Although they do not have the finesse of the naturally-aged product they nevertheless have a pleasant, refreshing taste.

Brewers who would like to try their hands at brewing Oud Bruin should have a good dose of patience in reserve. The best way to start is to acquire some bottles of naturally aged, unfiltered *Oud Bruin*. The next step is to blend them with a young beer in a wooden cask, hoping that the microorganisms in the *Oud Bruin* will find your cask hospitable. If available, casks that have been used to mature sherry or port are quite appropriate. Attempting this in more than one cask increases your chances of success.

- Oud Bruin Profile -

Original specific gravity: 1.048–1.053 (12°–13.1° Plato)
Apparent final gravity: 1.008–1.010 (2°–2.5° Plato)
Apparent degree of attenuation: 78–83%
Real degree of attenuation: 63–68%
pH: 3.5–4.0
Acidity (as lactic acid): 0.2%
Bitterness: 5.5–7 HBU per 5 gallons; 15–25 IBU
Color: 12–16° L
Alcohol: 3.8–4.4% w/v; 4.8–5.2% v/v

A recent Belgian survey mentioned 34 different brand names of *Oud Bruin*. Trying to pinpoint similarities between them can be quite difficult. The only thing that they really have in common is that they are dark in color. Here again the color can vary from red to dark brown or almost black. *Oud Bruins* are usually bottled, but in the immediate area of the brewers they are quite often available on draft. Some breweries even export their draft beer. Carbon dioxide volume therefore varies quite a bit: expect from 1.5 to 3.0 volumes of CO_2. Filtered versions tend to be gassier and more uniform than bottle-conditioned versions.

A few of the more traditional brewers bottle their products in champagne bottles with only a cork stopper and wire braid. Depending on the age of the bottle, various CO_2 levels can be encountered. When bottled they should be stored horizontally so that the cork will remain wet and keep its efficiency as a closure. I have encountered bottles that have lost their carbonation because they were improperly stored in a vertical position. The final gravity should be approximately one-quarter of the original gravity. They should not be too highly attenuated because the proper acidity level requires a small level of residual sugar to balance it.

The aroma of the *Oud Bruin* varies tremendously from brand to brand. The difference in aromas is brought on by the yeast used in primary fermentation and by the various microorganisms and bacteria encountered in the maturing or aging process. Some have a malty, sweet aroma, others have a distinctive acidic aroma. Aromas of port and sherry are quite common, more so in aged bottles.

It is probably easier to list aromas you will not encounter. *Oud Bruin* never gives off hoppy aromas, nor does it exhibit aromas common to other dark beers such as bock, brown ale, porter and stout. The aroma of dark malts such as black patent malt, roasted barley or even chocolate malt used in the brewing of these styles does not occur in *Oud Bruin*. The aroma can be fruity and floral. This reflects the yeast used. Diacetyl, caused either by fermentation or bacteria, is unacceptable. The bacteria that creates the fruity, acidic aromas do not produce diacetyl. Aromas from spices, alone or in blends, are not encountered.

Oud Bruin is sometimes aged with raspberries or cherries. Liefmans Frambozen Bier and Kriekbier are perfect examples. In such beers, the natural tang of the fruit blends with the acidity of the beer to create a completely new taste explosion.

Even without fruit, *Oud Bruin* exhibits a fruity palate. The acidity created by the bacteria, in conjunction with the yeast, in all cases dominates any bitterness caused by hops. Not all beers in this style exhibit this acid taste, though. Some beers have much lower acidity levels than others, causing a rounded fullness of taste complemented by an almost sweet, fruity finish and a low level of bitterness. There should never be a taste that can be directly traced to the hops. Therefore, hops with a low flavor profile are a must. Some brewers use old hops to ensure that no significant hop flavor is present in the finished beer.

A lot of the color in *Oud Bruin* is from long boils and, at times, slow cooling. These are the same practices frowned upon by Pilsener brewers because they are responsible for darkening the color of their beer. Brewers attempting to brew beers in this style should not use any malt darker than chocolate malt and only in small quantities. Crystal malt of the darkest color available is preferred. Although water of various compositions is used in the production of these beers, the resultant beers should show no significant level of dryness or lingering bitterness as from highly mineralized waters. The salty mineral finish encountered in stouts is very inappropriate.

Note: There exists in the neighboring Netherlands a style of beer also known as *Oud Bruin*. These beers are in no way comparable to the Belgian version. They are, as their name implies, brown or reddish in color. However they have a very low alcohol content, varying from 2 to 3 percent v/v and 1.6 to 2.4 percent w/v. They are not well-known outside of the country, although every brewer in the Netherlands seems to brew one. Never having sampled them, I cannot comment in detail.

3

Brewing Belgian Beers–Materials and Equipment

INGREDIENTS

- Sugar -

Most small brewers in North America pride themselves on brewing beer with only malt, water, hops and yeast in the centuries-old German tradition. So it may come as a shock to know that the majority of Belgian specialty brewers use sugar in various forms in crafting their product. The use of sugar in Pilseners and ales with alcohol content of 4 percent w/v (5 percent v/v) is not common, but sugar is almost a necessity in high gravity brews.

Fermenting an all-malt wort with a specific gravity of 1.070 or higher is uneconomical and unnecessary. The flavor, aroma and taste of the malt is not enhanced by having additional extract be malt. As a matter of fact, it contributes a heavy taste. Because the great majority of Belgian specialty beers are lightly hopped, this is unsuitable. On the other hand, sugars at this stage will lighten the taste while increasing the ethanol content. The resulting beer will be more drinkable and refreshing. Even small brewers who make hand-crafted, specialty beers use sugars. For the Belgian brewer, sugar in its various forms is as much a part of quality raw ingredients as malt, water, hops, and yeast—and many will proudly say so on their label. Most people drinking Belgian specialty beers remark on their lovely aroma. One of the constituents of this aroma comes from use of various brewing sugars.

Sucrose syrup derivatives are the most commonly used brewing sugars in the Belgian brewing industry. The use of corn-derived sugar such as glucose is now increasing, but a strong local industry of sucrose transformation from cane sugar exists while corn-derived products are quite often imported.

Sucrose comes from either sugar cane, grown in tropical areas, or sugar beet, grown in temperate areas, mainly Europe. The raw cane or beet is processed to remove impurities and reduce its water content. The resulting raw sugar is made up of about 95 percent sucrose and a small quantity of insoluble impurities. From its country of origin, it is shipped to various processors to refine it further.

Raw sugar is seldom used by brewers. Its degree and type of impurities varies from batch to batch and further refining is necessary in order to obtain a product of known qualities. Most people think of refined sugar as the white crystals sold in bags at the supermarket, but the brewer gets it in liquid form.

When the raw sugar arrives at the refinery it is again processed in order to clean it of its impurities. Most of these processes take place with the sugar in liquid form. After most of the impurities have been precipitated, the remaining liquid sugar undergoes evaporation in a vacuum. This evaporation is the same process that is used in the manufacture of malt extract. The only difference is that the liquid being processed is a sugar solution instead of wort. The sugar is reduced to a maximum of 65 percent concentration by weight. This is controlled very carefully because liquid sugar starts to crystallize at 67 percent w/w. Because it is still liquid, it must be used quickly. Wild yeasts are always present and can go to work at room temperature, imparting off tastes. However, it is more convenient to handle in liquid form, because it can be added directly to the brew kettle without danger of burning or caramelizing on the heating surfaces. As a disaccharide, sucrose is not readily fermented by yeast. It has to be hydrolized (broken down by reaction with water ions) to change into glucose and fructose which are fermentable. At that point, it is 95 percent fermentable, with some remaining impurities. Its pH in liquid form is around 7 to 7.5. It is light in color and has a nitrogen content of around 0.01 percent. Large, commercial brewers must do a careful nitrogen analysis to achieve a balanced nitrogen content in the wort when using sugar in worts of 10° to 12° Plato. When brewing a high-gravity wort this is less of a problem because the all-malt portion of the wort contains enough nitrogen to support a strong fermentation. Yeast nutrients in the form of amino acids are in more than sufficient quantity in worts above 1.060, and no problems of dilution are encountered.

Most brewers prefer to use invert sugar but sucrose syrup is sometimes used. Invert sugar is prepared through hydrolysis of sucrose. Various chemical processes are involved and the resulting liquid is again concentrated under vacuum pressure. The syrup contains around 49 percent dextrose, 49 percent fructose, and 2 percent sucrose. The reason it is called invert sugar is that a solution of invert sugar rotates a ray of polarized light to the left. Sucrose rotates it to the right, as does glucose. Fructose (or levulose, as it is also called) rotates it to the left. The left rotation of fructose is stronger than the right rotation of glucose so that the two sugars in combination rotate the beam to the left. In other words, it inverts the ray of light from right to left. This is why it is called invert sugar.

Although he did not do extensive research on sugars, Louis Pasteur did fundamental work on this aspect of light rotation. In 1848 Pasteur had just received his doctorate of science degree at the age of 25. One of his first research projects was to analyze the salt deposit of racemic acid found on the bottom of wine casks. This salt was known to be similar to the salt of tartaric acid, a salt that twisted polarized light. But a salt of racemic acid did not twist the light. One day Pasteur looked under the microscope at a dried up solution of racemic acid that had been left on the shelf. His inquisitive eyes saw something that others had never seen before. There, under his eyes, were two different forms of crystals, just like a pair of gloves: right hand ones and left hand ones. With tweezers and patience he separated them with the aide of the microscope. He then made a solution of the right hand ones and another of the left hand ones. When submitted to polarized light, the left hand ones rotated the light to the left, and the right hand ones to the right. When he mixed the two solutions together they did not twist the light.

This original research by Pasteur is equally as fundamental, although not as well known as his microbiological research. During that period this strange phenomenon was not completely understood. Chemical analysis through optical activity is now commonly used in research. Although it was by accident that the racemic salt solution had been left to dry out, Pasteur's curiosity prompted him to have a look at it. He was later to coin a phrase that sums it all up: "In the field of observation, chance favors only the prepared mind."

The pH of invert sugar can vary from 4 to 6. It can be made in various colors and it ferments almost completely, although the darker syrup ferments a little bit less completely than light-colored ones. The components responsible for coloring also contribute to specific flavors. Invert sugar contains about the same amount of nitrogen as sucrose.

Priming sugar solutions are quite often of a mixture of sucrose and invert sugar. A mixture of 55 percent invert sugar/45 percent sucrose is quite stable. It does not crystallize easily and has an extended shelf life. Blends can be made that will give different flavor profiles and color. Syrups can also contain different levels of fructose, a component of invert sugar. Fructose gives a sweeter taste than sucrose. Invert sugar is a popular priming sugar for bottle-conditioning in Belgian breweries.

Belgian brewers do use sucrose or invert sugar syrups, but most still prefer to use candi sugar, in either solid or syrup form. *Candi* sugar is made by the slow crystallization of a highly concentrated hot sugar solution. The sugar solution is cooled in a tank in which cotton strings are hung. The crystals form themselves around the strings. The slower the cooling, the larger the crystals become. White candi is obtained from a colorless sugar solution, while colored candi is obtained from a caramelized sugar solution. *Candi* is made up of 99 percent dry matter, and it contains 99 percent sucrose. It is very pure sugar because of its slow crystallization process. The crystals can measure from one-half to three-fourths of an inch (1 to 2 cm). They are hard and look like pieces of broken glass. If kept in a humid environment they have a tendency to stick together, but they can be easily broken apart. In solid form *candi* stores well and is very simple to use. Just weigh and dump it in the brew kettle. It melts almost instantly. There is no need to stir and no danger of caramelizing on hot surfaces. It is claimed that *candi* contributes to good head retention in a high-gravity, lightly hopped beer. It is also reported that it helps blend taste with aroma, and that it also has its own characteristic sweet aroma.

Candi is also quite often used in liquid form. It is very convenient, especially for big breweries. They receive it in tankers, from which they pump it to reservoirs. With an accurate pump and flow meter they can add the exact quantity called for in a recipe. Pale *candi* syrup is much darker than sucrose or invert sugar syrup. Invert sugar syrup has a color of around 30 EBC while the light *candi* ranges from 300 to 425 EBC. The dark version is 1700 to 2000 EBC. Both the pale and the dark liquid *candi* contain around 45 percent sucrose. The pale has approximately 34 to 44 percent invert sugar, while the darker syrup contains 44 to 45 percent invert sugar. The pH of both these *candi* syrups varies between 5.5 to 5.9.

Note: For persons more familiar with the A.S.B.C. or Lovibond degree color, the following conversion formulas can be used:

A.S.B.C. or Lovibond degree color = EBC color x 0.375 + 0.46
EBC color = A.S.B.C. color x 2.65 – 1.2

Candi sugar is not commonly sold in North America. It is available in Belgium in 50 pound bags from brewery suppliers. Although brown sugar in various forms and colors can be used as a substitute it does not have the same taste profile. Brown sugar is a sucrose and does not ferment like a mixture of dextrose and sucrose.

-Malt-

Although every brewer in the world tries to substitute for it to some extent, malt is still the backbone of brewing.

All the high gravity beers produced in Belgium use adjunct in one form or the other, but the malt portion is still most important and Belgian brewers have many different types of malts from which to choose.

The most popular malt is the basic Pilsener malt. It is very similar to most lager type malt made anywhere in the world. It has a light color of 2 to 4 EBCs (2°L), having been kilned at a temperature of between 131 to 158 degrees F (55 to 70 degrees C). It is the malt most preferred for producing Tripples, and light colored beers such as white beers and various Specials.

For ale production some brewers will also add various amounts of pale-ale malt. These malts are commonly used in the production of British pale ales brewed under license in Belgium. It helps to produce full-bodied beers, while providing a certain degree of coloration. Pale ale malt is normally kilned at 185 to 194 degrees F (84 to 90 degrees C) to achieve a color of 7 to 9 EBC units (3-4°L).

Munich malt is also used in various quantities. It increases the aroma and body, and provides an increase in color. It is kilned at 212 to 221 degrees F (100 to 105 degrees C) yielding a color of 14 to 16 EBC (6°L).

For strong increase in aroma and body Aromatic malt is the choice. It is kilned to 239 degrees F (115 degrees C) and held there, until a color of 45 to 55 EBC units (17 to 21°L) is reached. It will give a darker coloration to the beer along with a more distinctive aroma.

Compared to caramel malt, all the malts mentioned above have strong diastatic power because of basically low kilning temperatures.

The world's largest producer of caramel malt is located in Belgium. To produce high quality caramel malt, only green malt is employed. Trying to make caramel malt by resteeping a kilned and dried malt results in a very uneven rehydration, and the subsequent liquefaction of enzymes and saccharification is very inconsistent. Green malt that has been germinated to produce caramel malt is put into large drums and mixed with water to achieve saccharification. Then steam is introduced to raise the temperature, and heat applied to caramelize the grains. The entire operation requires a tight control of the environment. Special rotating drums are required for this operation. The maltster does not hurry the heating process. Good caramelization takes place at around 356 degrees F (180 degrees C). Higher temperatures can produce a bitter grain. Properly-made caramel malts are said to possess high levels of amino acids and preformed sugars. They give the resulting beer high colloidal and organoleptic stability which, in simple terms, improves appearance and shelf life.

Today, four different types of caramel malts are produced: Carapils (10 to 20 EBC, 4 to 8°L) gives added body to light colored beers and is used mainly in Pilsener brewing. Caravienne (30 to 60 EBC, 12 to 23°L) is used in the brewing of lighter colored Specials and Abbey type beers. Caramunich or crystal malt (140 to 160 EBC, 53 to 60°L) has a definite coloring effect. Finally, Special B is a highly colored caramel malt of 300 to 500 EBC (113 to 188°L) and gives a rich caramel-malt taste. It is used in Scotch ales and stouts brewed under license in Belgium. Darker Specials and Abbey beers at times use this type of caramel malt. Its effect is noticeable in beers, giving lots of additional body and coloring. Beers using Special B have more well-rounded malt character than beers colored with only *candi* sugar.

Darker roasted malts are also available but are seldom used in typical Belgian recipes. The stouts and Scotch ales brewed under license are the principal users. Chocolate malt with an EBC coloring of 900 to 1100 (338 to 413°L), and roasted malt with an EBC color 1400 to 1600 (525 to 600°L)

Taking a break after shovelling the spent grain out of the mash tank at Brasserie Lefebvre in Quesnat. Photo by Jérôme Denys.

are typically used. Both these roasted malts are made from Pilsener malt, and are roasted at a temperature of 420 degrees F (220 degrees C) or higher. The maltster is just interested in producing a malt that will give color to the beer, and not in extract value. There is no saccharification and caramelization phase. Roasted barley is also produced with an EBC level of 1400 to 1600 (525 to 600° L) . It is used only in stout brewing. Brewers trying a hand at brewing specialty Belgian beers should be very careful in using coloring malts. They can be used to color various beers but they should never leave their typical bitter taste behind. Up to 0.5 oz (15 gr) per gallon should create no problem.

Although many of these malts are not available in North America, other available malts are quite suitable. My opinion is that brewers should use locally-made products whenever possible in their recipes. Ordinary two-row malt can be used as the backbone of any recipe with various combinations of caramel and Munich malt to complement. Color correction can be achieved with darker sugars and minimal quantities of coloring malt.

- Hops -

Hops have been cultivated in Belgium since the 15th century. Historians believe that Flemish immigrants from what is today Belgium, introduced hops to England. Hops are currently grown in the Flanders region of Belgium. Old brewing text books have always praised Belgian hops from Alost and Poperinge. It is unclear what was grown years ago but nowadays production has declined tremendously.

The year 1986 was a good year worldwide for hops growing and as a result market prices were soon depressed. The market prices were so low that farmers from the Alost-Asse region in the Pajottenland gave up their hop culture. Nowadays there are only 85 specialized hop farmers in Belgium. The keikoppen (hard headed ones) are the most serious, farming 320 hectares in Westhoek, which is in the Poperinge area. Until recently the main varieties cultivated were Northern Brewer and Brewer's Gold. Now the farmers are replanting with new varieties such as Challenger,

Hersbrücker and Target in an attempt to get better prices on the market. Although Belgian hop production is small by world standards, its folklore is great. For example, every three years Poperinge hosts the Great Hop Festival. A parade with floats and more than 2000 participants is the main attraction. Additionally, there is a National Hop Museum open all year in Poperinge.

With such a small production base, no Belgian brewers rely entirely on native hops for their beers. The hops produced are not the favorite of the brewers either. Nowadays hop farmers do not sell directly to the brewers anyway. Instead, merchants around the world buy from hop farmers and in turn sell to the brewers. Bitter varieties such as the ones grown in Belgium are quite often processed into pellets and sold to the major brewers.

None of the brewers contacted showed a liking for the bitter varieties. They all have a definite preference for the aromatic varieties without regard to where they are grown. Different recipes will call for different hops. Ales can be brewed with a combination of Saaz from Czechoslovakia, Golding from England, and Styrian from Yugoslavia. A Pilsener brewer, Maes, uses only Saaz hops along with Czech malt in brewing the Maes Pils. American varieties such as Cascade and Willamette are totally unknown. Brewers trying their hand at Belgian taste should refrain from using these hops. Bitter varieties can be used cautiously. As a rule, they should not contribute a hop flavor (see Recipes, Chapter 5, for more information).

Belgian beers of all kinds are always lightly hopped. Traditionally, brewing such beers as Lambic and White beers has always called for hops aged one to two years. The brewers wanted the preservative qualities of the hops and not their bittering qualities. Also lots of hops in the brew kettle help coagulate proteins.

From the hop quantity given in the recipes you will understand what is meant by low bitterness values. This represents at least half the values usually given for pale ales and such. Brewing these recipes and fermenting them with a good Belgian ale yeast will let you taste exactly what is meant by hops as a complement to the other flavors present in a fine Belgian beer.

The following hops are good choices for bittering and aromatic finishing:

Variety	Alpha acid %	Bittering	Aroma
Hallertauer	4–6	yes	yes
Hersbrucker	4–6	yes	yes
Saaz	2.8–4.5	yes	yes
Styrian	4.5–6.5	yes	yes
Tettnanger	3.5–5	yes	yes
Perle	7–9	yes	no
Golding	4–6	yes	yes

The alpha values shown are lower than those usually given, but they are more realistically the values of the hops as you receive them. The "as cropped" alpha values are rarely encountered by the amateur or microbrewer. Furthermore, with the low-alpha Acid varieties, errors are less drastic than with the highly bitter varieties.

Let me emphasize again that should you want to create a hoppy special or abbey beer you should not hesitate, as it can be truly within the style. But make sure that you use a hop with lots of hop flavor and aroma and not a hop with only high bittering value. Good examples of hoppy beers are: Cuvée de l'Ermitage, an abbey beer by Brasserie Union, and Oerbier by the Dolle Brouwer. The first one is truly a well-rounded strong abbey beer with lots of hop flavor and a dry finish. The second is a bit heavier but with a complex malt, hops, and chocolate nose, followed by a mellow flavorful hoppy taste and a faintly lingering bitter aftertaste.

BREWING EQUIPMENT

One of the most amazing things about Belgian specialty brewers is the great variety of equipment used. At the turn of the century, every village had a brewery. Local beer styles were abundant. During World War I, Belgium was quickly occupied by German troops. One of the first things the invaders did was confiscate all equipment made out of copper. Within a year, almost all Belgian brewing equipment had been melted to make cannon shells. This fact, plus a rationing of the raw material, meant the demise of many smaller brewers. When the hostilities had ceased and peace was on the horizon many chose not to reopen. Those that did sometimes could not afford brand-new copper vessels. Old equipment that had been previously discarded was sometimes reintroduced.

- Mash Tanks -

At the turn of the twentieth century mash tanks made of steel were quite prevalent. These were large, open vessels with a motor-driven, central-rotating, mixing device. This large mixer kept the mash temperature uniform and was used in infusion mashing. Most often a central steam generator was the power source for these belt-driven devices. Sometimes these mash tanks were equipped with a false bottom, often made of bronze. Other times a separate lautering vessel was used.

Mash tanks were insulated with all kinds of materials; wood, cork panels, bricks, and tiles. Sometimes curtains were drawn around to prevent heat loss. Straw was thrown

An old lauter with a false bottom and cutting arm at the Lindemann Brewery. Perforations in the wheels allow wort to pass through into the hollow arm. Wort can get drawn off through the false bottom and perforated wheel. Photo by Eric Warner.

over the top of the mash to insulate it from the surrounding air.

Some of the tanks were directly fired by coal. Most of these have been discarded but some traditional craft brewers still swear by them and would not replace them for any reason. Brewers as a whole are very traditional and a taste of their beer quickly tells you that they are probably right. Although modern, stainless steel mashing vessels are easier to maintain and less labor intensive, they do not by themselves ensure a better beer. The art and craft of the brewer and the care he puts into his equipment is more important than the newness of the equipment.

Today, most Belgian specialty beer is mashed with an *infusion* method and top-fermented. Many of the same brewers also produce a Pilsener or export beer for their local market. These bottom-fermented beers are usually mashed with a traditional decoction method. Specialty brewers are usually medium-sized with a yearly output of between 25,000 barrels (30,000 hL) to 100,000 barrels (120,000 hL).

To accommodate both mashing methods they must have sophisticated equipment. The mash tank is made either of copper or of stainless steel. Some are directly fired

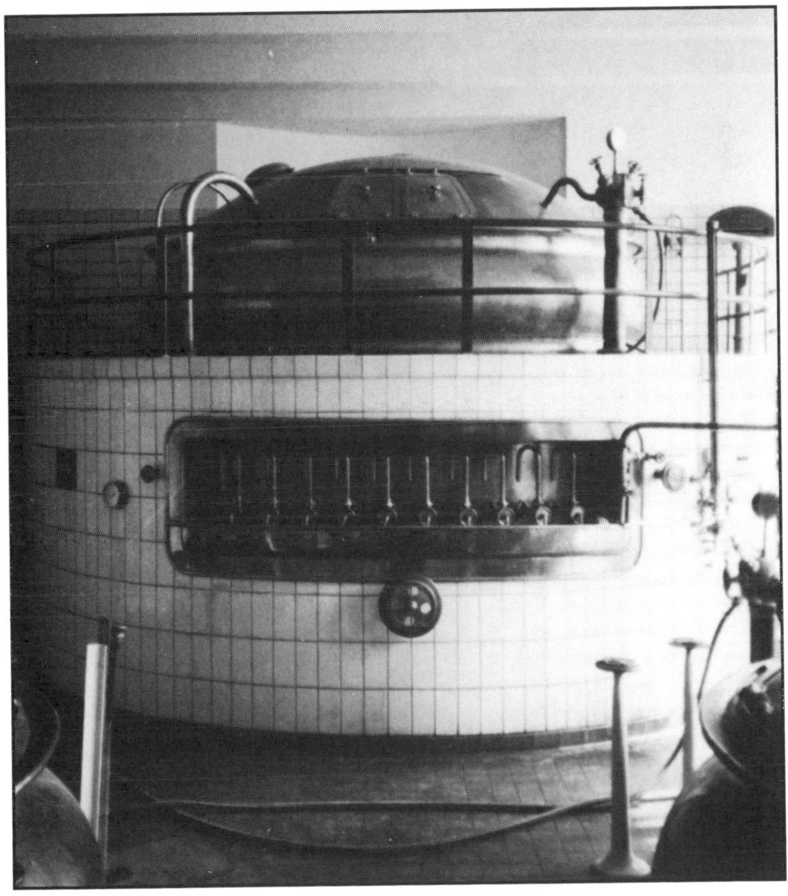

Gleaming tile clad copper lauter tun at the Huyghi brewery in Melle. Photo by Jérôme Denys.

Mash tank at the Dubisson Brewery in Pipaix. Note the mash filter in the background and the crushed malt hopper. Photo by Jérôme Denys.

by natural gas, or steam-heated through a jacketed outer shell. In some breweries the temperature of the whole mash is raised by adding near-to-boiling water.

Some of the mash tanks have incorporated false bottoms and others use a separate lautering device. The sparging of the grain is accomplished in a traditional lauter tun or in a device called a mash filter. This device receives the whole mash pumped onto a plate with a frame filter especially constructed for sparging. There the mash is held in place between filter cloths and pressure is applied. The wort is then automatically filtered and the necessary sparge water added. Modern versions of these filters are completely automatic and are said to deliver a very clean wort in less time than traditional devices.

- Brew Kettles -

Brew kettles come in all kinds of shapes and materials. Copper is still widely used and the most popular. Larger breweries who have purchased new equipment tend to favor stainless steel. Some breweries have brew kettles with no vents or chimney to direct the kettle vapor outside. Needless to say, the smell of wort is quite noticeable in those breweries. Under the kettle, all kinds of heat sources are used: steam, gas, and even coal shoveled by hand. Some brew kettles have rotating paddles inside to prevent caramelizing of the wort.

Both pellet and whole flower hops are used. After the boil the hot wort is usually put through a centrifuge to separate it from the hot break and the pellets. When whole hops are used the hop residue is usually squeezed in a special device to wring out the last drop of wort. Under Belgian law, the beer becomes taxable right after the boil, therefore every effort is made to retrieve or keep wort on which the brewer has already paid taxes.

- Wort Cooling -

Although plate-type heat exchangers are now quite commonly used, traditional brewers still rely on the open Beaudelot wort cooler. None of the brewers I visited used pure oxygen to aerate the wort; they all relied on filtered air.

After a second cooling, the slow fermentation starts in open tanks. During this fermentation period, the yeast mounting to the surface is skimmed off daily. At the end of this fermentation, this mash has turned into beer. Photo courtesy of Leifmans Brewery.

- Fermenters -

Fermentation takes place in all kinds of vessels. Larger breweries rely almost exclusively on cylindroconical fermenters. These are usually large enough to be installed outside. Being totally insulated and jacketed with glycol systems, they can be cooled or even warmed to adjust the ambient temperature. Some of them require two consecutive days of brewing to be filled. The majority of these fermenters are used in the production of ales. One major brewery uses them for production of Abbey beers.

However, many of the yeasts employed in high-gravity fermentations are totally inappropriate for use in cylindroconical fermenters. They rise to the surface and stay there after fermentation instead of settling on the bottom of the cone to be removed. Furthermore, these yeasts are usually skimmed after two days of active fermentation to be repitched in fresh wort. Because of this practice, successful small- and medium-sized brewers still have a preference for large, open fermenters. The size of these tanks is quite variable and so is the material used in their construction. Some brewers have large concrete tanks with an enameled interior. The fermentation temperature is controlled by pipes or plates submerged in the wort. Many brewers have no control over the primary fermentation temperature, and temperatures of 86 degrees F (30 degrees C) are frequent and normal for many brewers. Many brewers use covered, flat-bottomed, stainless steel vessels. Other brewers have enameled, mild steel vessels while, like Liefmans, ferments its Goudenband in large, open, copper fermenters. Fermentation is a domain that is really subject to tradition.

The following story shows what is meant by innovation based on tradition: The Dubuisson brewery in Pipaix is well known for its unique product, BUSH 12° strong beer. The beer is available in the United States under the name SCALDIS. A while back, Dubuisson looked into the possibility of fermenting their beer in cylindroconical fermenters. They ran test brews and had their product analyzed and tasted by a professional taste panel. They found that they could not achieve the same taste profile as when the beer was fermented in traditional, open fermenters. So instead of modernizing with conical fermenters, they had new, covered, flat-bottomed, stainless steel vessels fabricated.

For secondary fermentation many brewers rely on closed, cylindrical, enameled or stainless steel vessels. Secondary fermentation takes place at various temperatures. Some brewers keep the beer at 60 degrees F (15 degrees C) while others bring it down to almost freezing. Beer in

Belgium is never served at freezing temperatures. Therefore brewers are not as concerned with chill haze formation and removal. Belgian specialty beers left in a refrigerator are bound to develop chill haze.

Treatment before and after bottling varies from brewer to brewer. The larger ale breweries, subsidiaries of the major brewing groups, usually filter and pasteurize their beer. Centrifugal filters are frequently used. Pasteurization either takes place as flash pasteurization before bottling, or pasteurization in the bottle. The great majority of traditional beers are still bottle-conditioned, however. This is a field where Belgian brewers have attained a mastery that is unequaled anywhere else in the world.

4

Brewing Belgian Beers–Processes

BREWING WITH A BELGIAN MASTERBREWER

One of the brewers who contributed technical information to this book is Pierre Gobron who runs La Brasserie d'Achouffe, a small Belgian craft brewery. He is a relative newcomer to the Belgian brewing scene. Pierre brews high quality specialty beers three times a week in batches of 12 barrels (16 hL). All his beers are refermented in champagne bottles and sold in Belgium as premium beers. They are exported to Italy and the Netherlands. Over a third of his production is exported to Quebec where it has found favor with sophisticated beer drinkers. So when I asked specific questions regarding his brewing methods and recipes he suggested that we sit down and write a special recipe for this book! Furthermore he said, "Let's brew it together." So when he came to visit North America, we used my pilot brewery equipment and brewed a one-barrel batch of special Belgian-style high gravity beer.

The process and ingredients described here are similar to the recipe "Chou-Chou;" see Chapter 5. His first inquiry regarded the water to be used. At his brewery in the

Ardennes region, there is a spring flowing just behind the brewery. This is where he gets his water.

My advice to brewers is to adapt their brewing style and recipes to the water that they have. My water is very soft with a pH of 5.7 and I don't add anything to it. The prime quality of brewing water is that it should taste good. I do not like hard water that contains mineral salts. Because the beers that I brew are lightly hopped the ensuing beer would probably have a residual salty note to it if the water was hard.

He advises brewers who use city water to always filter it to remove the chlorine taste and compounds. He finds himself very fortunate to be in a mountainous area and have access to good brewing water. Other brewers in Belgium are not so fortunate, especially in the flat areas of Flanders. They have to check their water very carefully because the surrounding countryside is farmed intensively and, sometimes, overuse of chemical fertilizer can leach nitrate into the ground water.

To brew this recipe we brought in 40 gallons of very soft spring water. We checked the pH: it read 6.0. Although we had no chemical analysis done on the water, Pierre was quick to point out that it had a pleasant taste very similar to his.

All the beers I brew are made exclusively with pale 'pils-type' malt. I do not use any crystal or coloring malts. I find that they add too much of a residual taste to the beer. If I brew a darker-style beer like the Scotch-type MacChouffe I use dark *candi* sugar to get the nice amber color. I tried once to get the color with chocolate malt, but the taste was not as clean.

For this recipe we decided to use 70 pounds of two-row pale malt and add brown candi sugar in the brew kettle.

The best way to make a high gravity beer is to make a

thick mash. This way you do not dilute the sugars too much. Let me describe my installation and the way I go about it.

My mash tank is a dual purpose vessel and situated on the second floor. I do the whole mashing operation in it, and then I transfer by gravity the whole mash to a lautering vessel situation on the ground floor. The mash tank has a capacity of 425 gallons (16 hL). It is a single-wall vessel fabricated in stainless steel. The outside and the top are covered with mortared concrete blocks. This is a very cost effective way of insulating. Underneath is located a natural gas stove. I use the stove to heat the mash and raise my temperatures. To prevent scorching and caramelizing, there is a rotating paddle inside. During the whole mashing period it turns slowly at 30 revolutions per minute.

Because I make a very stiff mash, one quart of water to one pound of malt (one L of water to 500 g of malt) it has to be kept rotating all the time to even out the temperature. I have the heated brewing water ready at 140 degrees F (60 degrees C) and we slowly dump in the malt. The rotating paddle does a nice mixing job, and as soon as all the 550 pounds (250 kg) are in, the temperature is uniform at 136 degrees F (58 degrees C). With the gas heater I slowly raise the temperature to 145 degrees F (62 degrees C). It takes about 15 minutes and then I let it stay there for another 15 minutes. Then, I raise it to 151 degrees F (66 degrees C) and let it stay there until the starch conversion is completely done. Next, I raise it to 160 degrees F (70 degrees C) and let it rest 15 minutes. Finally, I raise it up to a final temperature of 169 degrees F (76 degrees C). The whole mashing program takes about 2 1/2 hours to complete.

Then the whole mash is emptied by gravity in the lautering vessel located below. As soon as it is in, I let it rest a few minutes and I start to recirculate the wort with the pump. Fifteen minutes is all that is required. This gives me just enough time to empty the mash tank of the spent grains and clean it. When it is ready I pump out the wort. It has a specific gravity of 1.087 (21° Plato). I pump most of the wort out and let the grain settle to the bottom. Then with a long-handled spoon I make a criss cross pattern on top of the grain bed. It is only then that I add sparge water. I cover the bed with about an inch of water and then I pump this first lautering to the brew kettle. I repeat this operation four times, until the brew kettle has reached its capacity of 12 barrels (16 hL). All the time that this is going on, the rotating paddle is working to prevent carmelizing and it is kept going throughout the boil. The extract content of the wort will vary between 1.066 to 1.080 (16.5 to 20° Plato), depending on the recipe. At this stage I add brewing sugars. In all my recipes I add glucose, which is sugar made from corn, and when I want to color the beer I add dark brown *candi* sugar.

The greatest difficulty we encountered when making this recipe was in heating the mash. Because the mash vessel was not equipped with a rotating paddle stirring was more tedious. With stiff mash, stirring with a long-handled shovel requires constant attention and effort. Because the stirring is done by hand, the cover on the mash tank is open all the time and heat is lost. So, getting up to the proper temperature took more time than we expected. Throughout the mash we took mash pH readings with a pH meter. It read 5.3— a figure that Pierre says is the same as his. After an iodine test showed that the starch conversion was completed, we added eight gallons (30 L) of 194 degrees F (90 degrees C) water to loosen up the mash and facilitate raising the temperature to the final 169 degrees F (76 degrees C) for mash off. This addition of water created an equilibrium temperature of 162 degrees F (72 degrees C) and, by heating the mash tank and recirculating, the final temperature was attained in 25 minutes. The whole mash was kept at 169 degrees F (76 degrees C) while the wort was recirculated for about five minutes, after which time it was clear. It was then pumped into the brew kettle. The specific gravity was 1.080 (19° Plato). Using the same procedure as at La Chouffe, the mash was completely drained and the top of the grain bed was criss crossed. Sparge water at 170 degrees F (76 degrees C) was added to cover the grain bed and the first lautering pumped into the brew kettle. Because the mash had been diluted, the grain was only sparged twice until 33 gallons (125 L) had been collected. The specific gravity was 1.076 (18.4° Plato) and the wort was quickly brought to boil.

I do not like my beers to be hoppy. I believe that a smooth taste is more important. When I want a hoppy beer my taste goes to an abbey-style beer like La Cuvée de l'Ermitage or a British pale ale like the ones we have in Belgium. I don't know why the British send us their best beers. I have at times tasted British beer in England and they were not as tasty as the ones we have in Belgium, although they were made by the same brewers. Compared to what they send us, they seemed more watery and of very low gravity. In my beers I usually employ three kinds of hops. For bittering, my preference goes to the Styrian from Yugoslavia and the Goldings from England. Although they have a low level of alpha acid they impart a fresh, smooth bitterness which blends well with the high alcohol content of my beers. As an aromatic hop, my present choice goes to Saaz from Czechoslovakia. All the hops I use are pellets. I find that they keep better and are easier to clean off after brewing.

When making this special recipe we followed Pierre's hopping schedule but with a slight change in the hops. As soon as the wort came to a boil, of 2 ounces (55 g) of 4.9 percent alpha acid Styrian hop pellets were added. One-half of an hour later, we added another 2 ounces (55 g) of

Styrian. After half an hour 2.2 pounds (1 kg) of brown candi sugar was added to the brew kettle.

This should raise the specific gravity by about 1.0035 (0.9° Plato) and give it a nice amber color.

An hour into the boil we added 2 ounces (55 g) of 4.5 percent alpha acid Hallertauer pellets. At the end of the boil, we added 3 1/4 ounces (90 g) of 3.6 percent alpha acid North Moravian whole hops from Czechoslovakia. To give it that special taste, 2 ounces (55 g) of crushed coriander seed was added to the brew kettle as soon as the heat had been turned off. As can be seen from this, the bitterness level in such a beer is quite low, but as Pierre is quick to point out:

Good beer should be a blend of tastes where no single component overwhelms the others. The result should be a unique smooth taste which reflects a blend of tastes. To me, a successful beer is one that contains many different aromatic and taste components, where not one predominates. With a judicious usage of spices one can come up with a unique taste that will have everyone guessing what is in it.

Right after the boil, the beer was decanted in a whirlpool tank and cooled immediately. A specific gravity reading showed a healthy 1.088 (21.1° Plato).

This means we had a good boil and the wort will be very clear. Because the yeast will be up against a high alcohol content half way through the fermentation, a healthy amount of yeast should be used. A minimum inoculant level for this type of beer should be at least 17.5 x 10^6 cells per mL.

To be on the safe side a quart and a half (roughly a liter and a half) of concentrated slurry was pitched in. The yeast had been previously obtained from Le Cheval Blanc, a Montreal brewpub that uses an ethanol tolerant yeast strain of Belgian origin. Because the amount of yeast used was large enough the wort was cooled to only 76 degrees F (24 degrees C) to insure a rapid start. A cylindroconical fermenter was used and the wort was pumped in through an inlet in the cover to aerate it vigorously. Four hours after the yeast had been pitched, it was already fermenting.

I like to ferment my beers at a high temperature. Sometimes it goes as high as 86 degrees F (30 degrees C). Fermentation should be over in less than a week. Four to five days is ideal. One thing that I do is to blend my beers during the main fermentation. Brewing three times a week makes this feasible. For example, on Monday I inoculate that brew with yeast that has raised to the top of the batch that I made the previous Wednesday. The Tuesday beer gets the same treatment. On Wednesday, I fill my third fermenter just partly and I add a portion of beer from the first and the second fermenter. The rest of the cooled aerated wort is added to fill the first and second fermenter. This ensures me of a vigorous fermentation. I can use my yeast for up to 20 weeks this way. I use open fermenters and my fermenting room is kept scrupulously clean. I am the only one that goes inside. It is sealed from the outside and the air that enters it has been filtered. When the fermentation is over, all three batches go into secondary aging tanks that are kept at 45 degrees F (7 degrees C). There it stays for a month before being bottled. Sometimes in export shipment, we bottle sooner because we know that the beer will have ample time to age and mature during its long voyage.

When asked what would be his advice to brewers who would like to try high gravity brewing, Pierre answered:

The most important thing is to make sure that you have a yeast that can do the work. This is very easy to find. You just need a small quantity of wort—let's say a cup. The wort can be all malt or malt and sugar. Your starting gravity should be around 1.080 (20° Plato). It can be either sterilized or hot packed, that is put in a jar when it is boiling. When it has cooled, you just shake the jar vigorously to aerate the wort. The yeast that you are going to test should come from a previous fermentation. You do not need much, about a tablespoon. Just add your yeast and let it ferment to completion. When there is no sign left of fermentation take the resulting beer from the jar and check it's specific gravity. It should be between 1.020 (5° Plato) and 1.012 (3° Plato). Expect the lower reading if you have added sugar to the wort. If it is only slightly above these readings, you should do the test again with more yeast. Be suspicious of anything over 1.025 (6.25° Plato). The yeast strain is probably not ethanol tolerant or a very slow fermenter. In this case, I would suggest that you try another yeast. The dry active yeasts on the market are not usually ethanol tolerant. My best advice would be to try the yeast from the bottom of a refermented Belgian beer. Just pour the bottom yeast deposit into a previously sterilized test tube or jar that contains approximately 10 to 20 mL of wort. The yeast should be active within 24 hours. If it takes longer it is probably weak, and I would not use it. I would then multiply it until I had reached a sufficient quantity to inoculate at least five gallons (20 L).

Our one-barrel batch took ten days to ferment down to 1.022 (5.6° Plato). A small heater was kept close to the fermenter to make sure the temperature would not fall below 72 degrees F (22 degrees C). Two cups of the wort were fermented separately with one-quarter cup of yeast to test the fermentation limit. It was kept at 80 degrees F (27 degrees C) for two weeks, and the specific gravity was checked. The reading was the same as in the fermenter. So the yeast was pulled from the bottom of the cylindroconical fermenter during the next two weeks and, when no further yeast could be removed, the beer was cooled down to around 50 degrees F (12 degrees C).

For bottling, a fresh yeast was prepared. It took three days from a slant to have two cups (500 mL) of wort actively fermenting. A priming solution made of wort and sugar was added along with the fresh yeast to the fermenter. The sugar content of the priming solution was calculated to be 2/3 ounce per gallon (5 g/L). After bottling, the beer was kept at 75 degrees F (24 degrees C) for two weeks. A first sample taste showed almost adequate carbonation. The aroma released from the beer combined esters with a touch of coriander, although yeast aroma was still present. The taste was admirably smooth but still green. A second sample taste three months later revealed outstanding aromatics but still some room for mellowing. It should improve with time and keep forever!

FERMENTATION

- Yeast -

When beer amateurs talk about high-gravity beers they think most often of barley wines. This brewing style is an art in itself; different than brewing high-gravity Belgian specialty beers. First, barley wines are usually made with a high-gravity wort, but not highly attenuated. This residual sweetness is balanced by adding a generous amount of hops in the brew kettle. The resulting heavily hopped and heavy-bodied ale is totally different from the lightly hopped and lighter-bodied Abbeys and Specials. The ingredient that allows higher attenuation is an ethanol-tolerant yeast strain with appropriate flavor characteristics. Belgians are very knowledgeable regarding such yeast strains.

Each brewery has one or more ethanol-tolerant yeast strains that they use. Brewers outside of Belgium have been known to use various wine or Champagne yeasts in fermenting high-density worts, but these do not have the aromas and tastes usually found in Belgian specialty beers. Although history does not record where these strains originated, we can understand how they became commonly used.

It has always been a custom in Europe to acquire yeast from another brewer if for some reason you encounter problems with your own. As a matter of fact, it is only in recent years that small breweries have cultured and maintained their own yeast strains. This is probably how ethanol-tolerant strains became widely used a few decades ago. When I visited small Belgian breweries in preparation for this book, two minor craft breweries who sometimes brew high-gravity beers, mentioned that they acquired the

The famous Rodenbach barrels proud centenarians. Photo courtesy of Rodenbach Brewery.

necessary yeast from a larger brewery in their region. Although most breweries do not offer or sell their yeast, some do.

In North America, exchange or sale of yeast strains may have been common a century ago, but today it is almost nonexistent. It is also probable that our yeasts would be totally inadequate for fermenting high-gravity worts. So the best way to get yeast for brewing a Belgian-type high-gravity beer is to culture a live yeast sample from a bottle-conditioned Belgian beer in a style similar to what you want to brew. The main prerequisite for success in this operation is to obtain a fresh bottle. This is quite difficult in North America but is worth a try. For instance, many brewers have been successful in culturing Chimay yeast. This Trappist beer has fairly good distribution, and fresh samples are often encountered.

The best way I have found to culture yeast is to pour a few cubic centimeters of the yeast at the bottom of a bottle into a test tube containing 10 mL of sterilized wort. Signs of fermentation should be visible in 24 hours. A slower start can mean two different things: either the sample was aged and therefore not vigorous or the sample might have wild yeasts that were used at some stage in the fermentation process. Unless you have access to a microscope and have had experience with slow starting yeasts, it is advisable not to use them. There is nothing more painful than dumping a batch that didn't start fermenting quickly enough. One sure way to failure is to use the method prescribed by some British authors: "Just pour the dregs from three bottles of bottle-conditioned beer directly into five gallons of wort." They add: "Fermentation will start overnight." This method might work in England where you can secure fresh beer, but trying it with bottles that might be months old is an invitation to disaster.

Actually the best way (although not always the most practical) is to bring back, or have friends bring back, fresh bottles purchased in Belgium. A note of caution: I have on many occasions encountered well-aged bottles that, although they were a sheer delight to drink, had yeast that was not viable. One of the best places to find fresh bottles is in supermarkets or shops that specialize in beer and soft drinks of all kinds. Beer specialists with a wide range of beers can be interesting, but ask the owner or person in charge about the age of the product before buying.

Once you have secured viable yeast you should test it for high-gravity brewing. The easiest way to do this is to make a few cups of wort from dried malt extract and obtain the specific gravity that you desire. Once cooled, add your yeast sample to the wort in a clean container with an airlock. Let it ferment to completion in a warm place. When fermentation is over, check the specific gravity. Yeast is viable if fermentation reduces specific gravity by at least 75 percent. For example, if the original gravity of your wort is 1.060, the fermented sample should be at least 1.015. Do not use any yeast that has not fermented at least three-quarters of the extract.

Many times, I have encountered ethanol-tolerant strains that have stopped fermenting with a high level of residual sugars. The reason is that all the yeast rises to the top. The yeast can be stirred back in with a sanitized spoon. This procedure, known as rousing, is quite frequent in British breweries which use similarly flocculent yeasts that have a tendency to "jump out" of the fermenter.

An easier way is to build up the yeast colony before pitching into a high-gravity wort. First pitch it into a wort of 1.040 to 1.050 (10° to 12.5° Plato). The yeast will easily ferment it down to 1.008 to 1.010 (2° to 2.5° Plato). Recover the yeast and repitch it in a high-gravity wort. You will then have enough yeast to ferment it completely in a few days. I have done this on many occasions and have regularly fermented worts of 1.090 (22.5° Plato) down to 1.022 (5.5° Plato) in six to seven days. To achieve successful fermentation a generous inoculum of fresh yeast is an absolute necessity. Two cups of fresh yeast per five gallons (500 mL/20 L) is a good target.

Many of the yeasts I have examined have been single strains. Sometimes two yeast strains can be found. One is a yeast used in the main fermentation; the second one is added at bottling for conditioning. Rarely will a mixture of two yeasts will be used in the main fermentation. Some brewers (such as the brewers of Trappist Orval) use two distinctive yeast strains in their process. The main fermentation is accomplished with one yeast, and takes place in open vessels in a climate-controlled room. When primary fermentation is over, the beer is transferred to large aging tanks. There, a second yeast of a wild ancestry is added. The beer stays in the aging cellar for one month with this new yeast, which gives it a particular taste and aroma. The aging cellar is kept at the unusually high temperature of 60 degrees F (15 degrees C). During this period, the beer is also dry hopped with fresh, whole flower hops. At bottling a priming solution is added, along with a fresh charge of the yeast used in primary fermentation. The beer is then kept for two months in large vaulted cellars until it is released for sale. Persons attempting to culture yeast from such a bottle can be either lucky or unlucky. To get an active primary fermentation the principal yeast must be present in greater numbers than the secondary yeast. The secondary yeast is notoriously a slow starter and also very powdery. Brewers attempting to ferment with these yeasts should have access to a microscope and be familiar with microbiological techniques.

As a rule, beers with a taste similar to other beers in a style use similar yeasts, which usually are of a single strain. Beers labeled by the brewer as a certain style but with a taste different from that style probably have something different in the yeast department. Let's take Orval as an example. It is a Trappist beer, but it tastes completely different than any other Trappist beer. Another example is the St. Idesbald Abdij beer. It is classified as an Abbey beer, but its taste and aroma profiles are more similar to lambic or Oud Bruin than to Abbey beer. It turns out that both Orval and St. Idesbald are fermented with an assortment of yeasts. Tripples are similar in taste, and most of them utilize single strain yeasts.

Many people have mentioned to me that Belgian beers contain unacceptable levels of bacteria. It is quite probable that investigation with a microscope proves this to be true, but taste should be the guiding factor. I have fermented worts with "bacteria infected yeast" and had excellent results. White beers will acquire a great acidic taste this way. Even strong beer can be beautifully balanced with a slight acidic aftertaste. The brewer making the beer should be the principal judge. Each time you do something different, you learn something new.

Achieving success with high-gravity fermentation is not accomplished overnight. Remember that breweries in Belgium are making these beers on a daily basis, with years of experience behind them. Their yeasts have become acclimated to each brewer's wort and environment. Brewers from other countries who want to make beers of a similar nature should arm themselves with patience and be prepared to experiment. Perseverance is the key to success in this field.

ESTER FORMATION

When someone tastes a strong Belgian beer such as a

Trappist or Special for the first time they invariably remark on the lovely fruity aroma that comes out of the glass. The major constituents of this aroma are esters. They are by-products of fermentation. Belgian craft brewers promote the conditions necessary for the production of high ester levels.

The high-volume Pilsener brewer is most concerned with producing a beer with low ester levels. Most of the current knowledge on ester formation is due to research done on how to reduce levels. The two most important esters produced during fermentation are iso-amyl acetate, with a taste threshold of 2 mg per liter, and ethyl acetate, with a taste threshold of 25 mg per liter. Ethyl acetate will definitely give fruity overtones at a level over 30 mg per liter. Iso-amyl acetate has been associated with banana flavors. Both of these flavor components are related to the strain of yeast used.

There are two major factors responsible for ester formation in brewing: wort gravity and dissolved oxygen level. The higher the gravity, the higher the resulting ester level. The higher the dissolved oxygen, the lower the ester level. High-volume commercial breweries doing high-gravity brewing never exceed a specific gravity of 1.060 because above that level the ester formation is too great for the style. When they dilute high-gravity beer with water at bottling (a practice becoming more common for cost savings), the aroma level is higher than when the beer is brewed at normal gravity.

A wort of 1.080 will result in a beer with an ester level four to eight times greater than a beer brewed with the same components at an original gravity of 1.040. So we can see that Belgian specialty beers with a starting gravity of between 1.060 and 1.090 will automatically result in highly fruity beer.

Fermenting a wort with an initial gravity of 1.045 with

a yeast used in a high-gravity beer of 1.075, would result in a beer with totally different aroma characteristics, even if the wort components are proportionally the same. Different yeast strains produce different aroma patterns, but their reactions to increased specific gravity are the same. They all produce beer with increased aroma levels at high gravity.

A commonly used practice of commercial brewers to reduce ester formation is to oxygenate the wort vigorously at yeast pitching, and sometimes even a few hours after. This practice works because the production of esters in fermentation is the result of a reaction between fatty acid material and alcohol. A closely linked component to this reaction is called acetyl coenzyme A. Depending on the molecular oxygen available, acetyl coenzyme A either participates in the biosynthesis of yeast fatty acids or in ester formation. The addition of molecular oxygen, either at yeast pitching or a while after causes acetyl coenzyme A to participate in yeast growth instead of increased ester formation.

None of the Belgian craft brewers I surveyed reported the use of pure oxygen to oxygenate their wort. All of them used either filtered or sterile air to aerate the wort. Test results have shown that if you saturate a wort of 1.080 original gravity with air at 60 degrees F (15 degrees C) you will obtain a dissolved oxygen level of 5.4 (mg/L). If you saturate it with pure oxygen you will get a level of 25.7 (mg/L). The oxygen level achieved with air saturation is barely acceptable for a normal fermentation. The recommended dissolved oxygen level for a good fermentation is between 8 and 10 mg/L. However, most of the craft brewers surveyed still used shallow, open fermenters where the wort comes in contact with air. A generous pitching of yeast also helps to overcome any difficulties from a low level of dissolved oxygen. None of the brewers reported problems with fermenting high-gravity beer that could be solved with an addition of oxygen. The result of this technique is a beer with a lots of aroma.

HIGHER ALCOHOL

High-gravity brewing produces beer with higher alcohol. These components contribute significantly to the flavor and aroma of the finished beer. They have flavor thresholds varying from as low as 10 mg/L to as high as 600 mg/L. Some higher alcohols, such as phenylethanol, can impart pleasant, fragrant aromas, while others produce bitter or solvent-like characteristics that are detrimental to the general flavor of the finished beer.

There are quite a few factors that significantly affect the formation of higher alcohols. The most important one is the yeast strain. Various tests have demonstrated that some strains produce greater amounts of higher alcohol than others. They also produce different higher alcohols from each other.

Because fermentation of a high-gravity beer usually takes place at high temperatures, excessive production of higher alcohols can occur. An increased pitching rate makes no significant excess, but a very vigorous aeration or oxygenation causes a remarkable increase in yeast growth, leading to increased higher alcohol levels. Without going into biochemistry, it is important to know that higher alcohols are the result of the metabolism of amino acids. The formation of amino acids is directly influenced by the level of available nitrogen in the wort. As a rule, an increase in the amount of available nitrogen will result in an increase in the formation of higher alcohols. But only up to a certain point. After reaching a peak, there is a decrease again. This can become very significant when using various nitrogen diluents such as sugars, glucose syrups, and even wheat flours. A nitrogen level of around 140 to 150 mg/L is usually satisfactory. Unless you use a large proportion of adjuncts, this level is usually obtainable.

Most of the Belgian brewers I surveyed believe their yeast strain is the most important factor for the flavor profile of their beer. The addition of brewing sugars can also have significant effects and can be used to give different flavor profiles to beer fermented with the same yeast. Fermentation under pressure is reported to lower the level of higher alcohols, but the majority of brewers still use open fermenters for their high-temperature fermentations.

REFERMENTATION IN THE BOTTLE TECHNIQUE

A recent survey which listed over 600 different brands of beers produced in Belgium, showed that at least 130 of those were refermented in the bottle. Refermentation involves bottling beer with a priming sugar and a fresh dose of yeast to produce natural carbonation. Although 130 is less than one-quarter of the total brands, these brands are a sizeable portion of the total volume exported from Belgium. When people think of Belgian beer, it is quite often in terms of beer with active yeast in it.

Although no one has proof, it is generally accepted that the first brewers actually to bottle with a fresh dose of yeast were the lambic brewers. Old brewing texts from early 1900s mention Gueuze as being the "Champagne of Brussels." In those days bottling and refermentation were sometimes chancy and flat beers were sometimes encountered. Lambic has always been a very temperamental beverage and difficult to handle.

At the beginning of the twentieth century, monks started to refine the bottling technique. For a long period they were the only ones to package traditionally brewed beers by refermenting in the bottle. But the success of their beers brought on competitors and very rapidly all brewers of strong, specialty beers began to use the technique.

There are quite a few technical advantages to method of bottling. First of all, the equipment required is less sophisticated and therefore less expensive than that required to bottle beer already carbonated. Because the beer has a yeast deposit at the bottom, the consumer knows that the beer will not be quite crystal clear. Although quite a few brewers do filter their beer through a centrifuge, some still rely on natural decantation before bottling. But most important, because the beer acquires its carbonation by natural means it ensures that the beer is a living beer. The beer is alive in the bottle and will follow a natural path of aging. The taste and aroma will change with time. Of course scrupulous sanitation is required. Clean fermentation is required, and bacteria free yeast is a necessity, unless the brewer decides that a judicious addition of bacterias will impart a definite taste profile to the beer. One of the major problems facing small brewers is the oxygen pick up that is almost inevitable in bottling, especially in filtered beer. Any oxygen picked up at this stage, will in all cases result in an aged, oxydized, cardboard taste. Unless a brewer has a state-of-the-art beer bottling machine he will encounter this problem with filtered beer. But when bottling living beer, the yeast actually uses that small quantity of oxygen to multiply itself and ferment. So unless the beer is badly handled and picks up too much oxygen, that premature aging taste will not occur.

Most brewers who have tried to filter beer realize how difficult it is to sterile filter the beer and then bottle in that aseptic condition. Because filtered beer has been stripped of all yeast it becomes a prime vehicle for bacterial infections. A minute quantity of bacteria in the filter can result in a catastrophe on the consumer shelf in a few weeks. Major breweries throughout the world have understood this problem for years, and although they have sophisticated bottling equipment and knowledgeable quality control personnel, the safest solution for them is to pasteurize their bottled beer. When bacteria have got the beer all to themselves they increase at an alarming rate in a medium that holds a good quantity of nutrients. But when bottling is done with a judicious addition of yeast, although the beer has been filtered, any bacteria faces stiff competition for nutrients. Unless the bacteria have been voluntarily added by the brewer, any minute quantity of bacteria stands very little chance of doing harm. Because the yeast population is overwhelming by comparison, it can consume all the nutrients and oxygen within a few hours of bottling and very little is left for bacteria. Of course bottling with viable yeast does not allow for sloppy brewing techniques. Quality control is as important and as necessary in high-volume production. However, for brewers bottling with yeast a slight slip is not quite as catastrophic as with filtered beer.

Homebrewers are quick to point out that they too have yeast in their bottle. The Belgian beers are no different, they quickly add. Up to a point they are right, there is yeast in the bottle, but the way it got there is quite another thing. Most homebrewers bottle beer that has aged for a while just by adding a certain quantity of sugar either directly in the bottle or as a liquid solution in the beer. Then they let it ferment again during a week or two and start enjoying the naturally-carbonated product. This is all nice and ok when dealing with beers of what we might call normal gravity; that is, beer fermented from a wort of 1.050 original gravity or lower. But what happens with a beer that has a content of eight, nine or even more percent alcohol per volume? Depending on the yeast that has been employed in primary fermentation, there is a good chance that it will referment a little bit and stay there. You end up with a beer with a very low carbonation level. On the other hand, notice how sparkling and lively a refermented Belgian beer is.

This phenomenon is quite understandable when you understand the lifestyle and habits of yeast. In order better to appreciate this aspect of fermentation we have to take a close look at what happens in normal brewery fermentation and what happens when you referment in the bottle. In normal brewery fermentation, yeast is added to oxygenated wort. The pH of the wort is around 5.1. At this stage the yeast picks up oxygen to build up its reserve, and when all the oxygen is depleted it starts to ferment. But what does it do with all that oxygen? To understand this we have to look at the construction of the yeast cell.

To better visualize, imagine that a yeast cell is just like a big inflatable balloon. To inflate a balloon you must add air through a valve and then close it. A yeast cell is the same. It has an outer cover just like a balloon, which we call the cell wall. This cell wall is made of different layers of different materials, the important one being the interior membrane called the cytoplasmic membrane. Through this membrane flows in all the necessities for a happy and healthy yeast life. But unlike a balloon which has a valve to close, there is not a single valve on the cell wall. The yeast cell must be kept in a proper environment so that all the nutrients flow in, are modified and the modified entities flow out again. In other words it must be kept elastic and healthy. To have elasticity or fluidity, phospholipids and triglycerids must be present. The yeast must either have them or be able to synthesize them. Normal beer wort contains all the necessary components in the form of lipids, saturated and unsaturated fatty acids that, with the help of enzymes and oxygen, synthesize the phospholipids and triglycerids. This is the major contribution of oxygen at the start of fermentation. When all the fermentable sugars have been assimilated, the yeast ceases to function and comes to rest on the top, or on the bottom or in both places. This is a normal course of events when brewing a normal gravity beer.

But what happens when you start fermenting a wort of a higher extract content? The yeast will start fermenting normally, but gradually as it encounters more and more alcohol, it will slow down. At a certain point it will stop fermenting completely. To combat this tendency, Belgian brewers have carefully selected yeast strains which are quite suited to ferment at high gravity and still produce beers with very desirable properties. What is different with refermentation in the bottle? First of all the yeast is faced with fermented beer, not wort. The pH instead of being at around 5.1 in wort is more likely to be below 4.4 and at times below 4. Whereas the wort is rich in nutrients and in saturated and unsaturated fatty acid, the beer is depleted. All these nutrients have been taken up by the yeast during primary fermentation. The yeast is also faced with a large quantity of alcohol, a media in which it is at best slow acting. And on top of it all, the yeast that is still present in the aged matured beer is in a pretty bad state. It has been deprived of nutrients for at least a few weeks and is slowly beginning to autolize or disintegrate its own cell walls. Basically, it is in a poor state of health. Brewers who just add sugar at this stage and expect to have a nicely bottle-conditioned beer in a few weeks are usually in for a surprise. Long ago Belgian brewers were faced with this problem especially when they started to bottle high-alcohol beers. They finally solved this problem by adding a fresh dose of yeast at bottling. But, you may ask, what kind of yeast do I need for this?

Practically speaking, this bottling system is used in commercial breweries who bottle on a day-to-day basis and always have beer at different stages of fermentation. But at what stage of the fermentation should bottling yeast be collected? As discussed previously one of the main requirements for healthy yeast is a permeable cytoplasmic membrane. For the yeast cell to absorb metabolites through its membrane, it must have a high energy reserve and a high enzymatic activity. In technical terms, it must have a high ATP (Adenosine triphophate) activity. It would be beyond the scope of this book to go into details of biochemistry, but suffice it to say that in a normal fermentation the peak of ATP activity is usually attained after 40 to 48 hours of fermentation. Even before this peak was established scientifically, German brewers had deduced that 40 to 48 hours was the right time to take their *kraüsen* or young fermenting wort used later in secondary fermentation. Thus for a commercial brewer it is a good practice to take this fresh yeast required for bottling during the second or third day of fermentation. Such yeast should also have good flocculation characteristics. Most of the bottle-conditioned beers have a yeast that really sticks to the bottom. Yeast in a healthy state will be more flocculating than yeast that has aged.

Another very important factor is the quantity of yeast that should be added. Experiments have demonstrated that a concentration between 100,000 to 500,000 yeast cells/mL provides an adequate refermentation. A higher inoculum will have a marginally quicker refermentation; however, the benefit is lost because the greater quantity of yeast present will, through aging and eventual autolysis, impart a harsher taste to the resulting beer.

Because this technique is used mostly with highly alcoholic beer, another important step that the Belgian brewers take is the so-called "Hot Room." As discussed previously, the yeast added to the finished beer at bottling is put into what we might call a competitive environment. It is very important that the yeast does its work quickly. As soon as the beer is bottled, labelled, and packed in boxes, it is put into the "Hot Room." This is basically a room with a controlled environment and constant temperature of 80 to 90 degrees F (27 to 32 degrees C). To achieve this temperature some breweries have radiant-heated floors. Basically it is a room where the beer will be kept at a constant warm temperature for usually two weeks. During this time the fresh yeast accomplishes its refermentation quickly and in a predictable manner.

A notable exception to this refermentation is the Trappist beer Orval. Like all the others it is bottled with a fresh dose of yeast but is stored in an immense cellar kept at between 60 and 70 degrees F (15.5 and 21 degrees C). There it is kept for two months to mature and age before being shipped. Do not forget that Orval is not a high alcohol beer (at only 5.2 percent v/v) and therefore the yeast can act more slowly without facing a high alcohol concentration.

Belgian brewers use different sugars at bottling. Some use *candi* sugar. If in solid form it has to be dissolved or, it can be purchased as a ready-made priming solution. Care must be taken to ensure that it is bacterially clean. Some brewers pasteurize their priming solution to be on the safe side. Sugar solutions are notoriously good carriers of bacteria. Others use invert sugar which is obtained in an easy-to-use liquid form. Invert sugar is directly fermentable by the yeast and ensures a rapid refermentation. Other brewers rely on a mixture of sugars. Some even have mixtures of glucose and other sugars. All this is in the so-called domain of brewing secrets and age-old recipes.

There are various suppliers in Belgium who specialize in priming sugars and fabricate mixtures according to the individual specifications of brewers. Most of these priming sugars are in liquid form and have a limited shelf-life because sugar in a liquid form has a tendency to crystallize. They must be kept at a specific temperature and used fairly quickly. For the small brewer the easiest one to handle is invert sugar. It has a fairly stable shelf-life and is usually available in five gallon quantities. In North America these sugars would probably be hard to find in small quantities. They are used by various candies and sweets manufacturers but usually sold in impractical minimum quantities. Unless a brewer specializes in large scale bottle-conditioning he is probably better off using powdered dextrose. Of course, for commercial production, the brewer is wise to pasteurize the priming solution before using it.

What about the brewer who does not brew regularly or might not have fresh yeast available? Although more labor intensive culturing can be done easily by any one with adequate experience in yeast handling. The best beers to practice these culturing techniques on are those with a regular gravity. A normal 5 percent v/v will not present any difficulty due to high alcohol level. Any brewing yeast usually employed can do the job readily. The easiest and most predictable way of doing this is with yeast on a slant. The operation should bc started 48 hours before the actual bottling date.

The brewer should have the following presterilized containers at his disposal: test tube containing 10 mL of sterilized wort and sterilized jars for 40 and 250 mL of sterilized wort. Using the appropriate sterile transfer technique, inoculate the 10 mL test tube with a needle of yeast from the slant. If the yeast is of adequate quality it should show signs of fermentation within 20 hours. If it shows no sign of activity discard it and acquire a new culture. As soon as it has started to ferment in the 10 mL tube it should be transferred using sterile technique into the 40 mL container.

Usually it will show signs of activity between the fourth to the sixth hour. It should then be transfered to the 250 mL vessel. Here again it will show visible signs of fermentation in about the same time. When the white foam cover on the fermenting beer gets to about a quarter of an inch thick the fresh yeast is at its maximum level of activity and should be used right away. The quantity of yeast present in this quantity is sufficient to referment properly a normal homebrewer's batch of five gallons. Depending on the yeast strain and vigour this addition will give a total value of between 100,000 to 500,000 cells per mL concentration in the beer to be primed.

This method of priming can also be used with dry active yeast. A quarter teaspoon is usually sufficient. The yeast should be rehydrated in water that has been warmed to at least 95°F and then added to sterile wort. Let it ferment until it gets to that quarter of an inch foam level and then use it just like the slant yeast. To minimize the dangers of bad yeast, attempt this only with a reliable yeast batch that has proven adequate. The total 300 ml volume of fermenting wort contains as unfermented wort the equivalent of approximately 20 gr of sugar. This should be taken into account when figuring out the total amount of sugar that will be used in the priming. At this stage the brewer should also add the proper amount of pasteurized sugar solution. The amount used should not be more than 2 to 2 1/2 oz per gallons units. When surveyed on their bottling methods, Belgian brewers answered differently when asked about the various amounts of sugars used in refermentation, and none of them seem to agree on a set figure. This is probably because they do not use the same priming sugar from brewery to brewery and what is satisfactory for one is totally inadequate for the other one. Brewers who try this method for the first time should use the same amount of priming sugar that they normally use. The beer will not have more carbonation than usual; it will just be properly carbonated more quickly.

Refermenting in the bottle is most rewarding when priming highly alcoholic beer. Of course the brewer should already have fermented his beer with an ethanol tolerant yeast strain. If that yeast gave a satisfactory fermentation, he should not hesitate to use it in refermentation. In this case he should also make every effort to keep his beer warm after it has been bottled to make sure that it referments quickly. When the proper carbonation level has been reached the beer can be stored in a cool cellar.

5

Recipes for Belgian Beers

RECIPE NOTES

Before reading and proceeding with the recipes, read in Chapter 4 "Brewing with a Belgian Brewmaster." All of these recipes have been tested—if you employ a top fermenting yeast of Belgian origin you can achieve a result comparable to a genuine Belgian beer. It is essential, however, that you use an ethanol tolerant yeast strain with the high gravity brews.

Suggested hops can be replaced by similar ones but not by more bitter ones. To get the same taste and flavor, do not overhop. If you use high alpha hops for bittering, use a precision scale to weigh them. The IBU given for the recipes are actual bitterness level quoted by brewers. The Homebrewers Bittering Units (HBU) were calculated to represent a 25 percent utilization factor.

In recipes with spices, the figure given is a guideline. You can increase or decrease to suit your taste. But as a rule their effect will diminish with time. So if you intend to age the beer you can use more spices, but not if you intend to drink it young. In the beer that should age, spices blend with the overall taste and create a new taste. A note of caution:

the recipe Santa Claus' Magic Potion calls for sweet gale seeds and nutmeg. Get a precision scale for these. Sweet gale was used in the brews of the Middle Ages and is a very powerful aromatic.

In calculating the original gravities of the beers it is assumed that you would get for every pound of malt used per gallon (120 g/L), a specific gravity reading of 1.030, when brewing five gallons. For the one barrel recipe, because of better extraction possibilities, a specific gravity of 1.035 for the same ratio of malt to water has been used.

Because Belgian beers are lightly hopped, do not use highly mineralized water. The only important value to obtain during mashing is a proper pH. Brewers should aim for a value between 5.2 and 5.4.

Boiling time should be at least one and one-half hours. If on your first try with one of the recipes you do not achieve the correct specific gravity you can raise the gravity reading by either boiling longer or adding a bit of sugar. It is assumed that a pound of sugar per 5 gallons raises the specific gravity by 1.008 (2° Plato) or 100 g of sugar in 20 liters raises the specific gravity by 1.002 (0.5° Plato). With regard to color, adding sugar raises the gravity without increasing the color; boiling longer increases the color somewhat.

Although sugar may be against some people's brewing purity code, the use of sugar is essential in obtaining tastes specific to the style. A 1.080 (20° Plato) Tripple made with all malt will not taste like a Tripple, although it will be an excellent beer. I agree that sugar has no business in beer below 1.048 (12° Plato) but it is necessary in high-gravity, Belgian-style beers in order to get the light taste. The quantity suggested in the recipes is a minimal amount anyway. Dextrose or corn sugar are good choices for a neutral sugar. Dark brown or demerara sugar can be used in darker-colored beers. Of course, if you can obtain candi sugar, it would be most authentic.

Two recipes, Oud Bruin and Silk Lady, call for using flour. This is the easiest way to recreate recipes that use raw grains. Milling and obtaining wheat or oats can be problematic. For these recipes, try to obtain in both cases whole wheat or oat flour. You can usually obtain them in a health food store. The only problem you may have with them is that they may clump if you dump them directly in the mash. Instead, just sift them over the mash slowly and mix evenly. Another easy way is to mix the sifted flour over part of the mash water and mix thoroughly. Then you just add this milky solution to the rest of the mash water. Flours can be up to 10 percent of the total ingredients without any problem. The enzyme in the malt easily converts the starch to sugars. Wheat or oat flakes sold in brewing supply stores can also be substituted.

For simplicity all the grain recipes are shown with a single temperature infusion mash. Depending on the equipment available, a step infusion (by raising the temperature either directly or with an addition of water) is also recommended. High gravity brews should have a malt-to-water ratio of one pound of malt per one quart of water (500 g/L). Do not oversparge.

The recipe "Driver's Choice" is a typical, low gravity beer like those available in Belgium. Although not praised, and relatively unknown, Belgian low gravity beers—known as *bière de table* (literally "table beer")—account for around 3.5 percent of the total production. They are classified as Category III beers, having an original gravity between 1.004 to 1.016 (1° to 4° Plato). Commercially they are brewed with the last runnings from the mash tank. Although the recipe is given, the intention is that when making a high gravity brew you sparge further and ferment the last runnings into a low gravity beer. Although some government authorities caution against pregnant women drinking beer, European doctors regularly recommend *bière de table* to pregnant women. An addition of crystal malt with dextrine powder gives more body to these beers. Hops are also increased to raise the taste level. Because of their low alcohol content, these low gravity beers should be consumed soon. The low extract level offers a low level of amino acids for yeast development, therefore the yeast employed should be the freshest possible and come from a previous healthy fermentation. After fermenting *bière de table,* the yeast should be discarded.

To get the proper taste in the Oud Bruin you must have the proper microflora at your disposal. Sometimes the yeast from a white beer, which has an interesting acidity level, can be used. To really do it right, you should brew this once and let it, or a portion of the batch, age for one year. When you have attained a suitable aged taste, brew again and blend the old with the new. The same technique can be employed with the recipe Grand Cru, as a substitute for the two yeast handling. If you cannot separate the two cultures in a mixed culture you can do it with the blend by doing it in steps. When you have a quart of culture actively fermenting, add it to no more than one gallon of wort. When you see signs of fermentation add two more gallons. After a few hours and renewed signs of fermentation add the rest. Some two-yeast combinations are quite often slow together and multiply slugglishly.

All the beers with a starting gravity above 1.063 (15.75° Plato) should be bottled because they improve tremendously with age. This is really the most interesting thing with brewing Belgian-type beer. When they are made properly, they improve a lot and the taste keeps on changing. One note of caution about bottling: the priming sugar recommended should never be exceeded, and brewers should make sure that their beer has fermented to the limit. Belgian brewers, at times, use more priming sugar than the level recommended here but they always use special bottles suitable for refermentation. Notice how thick the Orval bottle is. It is made to the same standard as a Champagne bottle. Try to bottle these high gravity beers in returnable bottles or at least premium bottles. Stay away from the so-called one way or non-redeemable bottles.

For bottling high gravity beers follow the recommendations outlined in Chapter 4, "Brewing with a Belgian Brewmaster." Try to keep the bottled beer warm for the first two weeks after bottling. When the beer is adequately carbonated, store in a cool cellar. There is always a renewal of fermentation in the summer and yeast in the bottle is always slower acting.

When ready to serve, keep the beer cool but not cold. If you have refermented with fresh yeast you may notice how the yeast sticks to the bottom of the bottle. Open the bottle and pour in one continuous motion into the glass. Although there are many types of glasses suitable for these beers, wide-open types are recommended. These glasses allow the beer to create a lively foamy head, letting it come alive without restraint.

USING MALT EXTRACT

Brewing Belgian style beers with malt extract is something that can be easily and readily done. As far as I know there are no malt extracts manufactured in Belgium. Brewing kits for making Belgian-style ales are sold in Belgium. I have also seen them in Canada and they are reportedly available in the United States. In Belgium, the label on the cans mentions that they are imported. I assume that they are manufactured in England. I have never used them and do not know of anyone who has. There are few homebrewers in Belgium anyway. With such an array of beers to choose from, you would have to drink two different beers every day to go "full circle" in one year. Beer is sold almost anywhere and the prices are reasonable.

All the recipes have been formulated on the assumption that malt extract used at the ratio of one pound per gallon (120 g/L) gives a specific gravity of 1.040. Variations can be expected but they are slight. Because a large quantity of extract is necessary to produce high gravity beers, it is recommended that you compensate the small gravity differences with sugars rather than with additional malt extract.

The malt extract recommended above is sufficient to have the full body of a Belgian beer. We must remember that a quality of the high gravity Belgian beers is their medium body. They must have a certain degree of lightness. Two ounces of sugar per 5 gallons (50 g/20 L) raises your specific gravity reading by 0.001. Make sure that when you adjust your reading, you have taken your specific gravity reading at the calibrated temperature for your hydrometer.

The extract recommended for the recipes is normal pale malt extract in either liquid or dry form. Because the color will vary from manufacturer to manufacturer you might have to adjust. You can easily accomplish this with crystal malt or colored sugars such as raw sugar, brown sugar or demerara sugar. The only two classes of Belgian beer restricted in terms of color are the Tripple and the white beers. With these you should aim at getting the color of a pilsener. Whatever extract you have used previously to brew a pilsener should work well to brew these styles. Because you use more extract in a Tripple, you can expect a darker color. However, additional sugar lightens the body and increases the gravity, bringing down your color to the right level. For white beer you can use pale wheat malt extract with ordinary pale malt extract to get the right color.

Unhopped malt extract is best. But if you want to use hopped extract you can do so, just do not add any more bittering hops. The hopped extracts are usually not aggressively hopped. Do not forget that, as a whole, Belgian beers are not highly bitter. Adding hops at the end of the boil is probably the only necessary hop addition.

Many recipes call for crystal malt. This gives a bit of body to extract recipes. There are no color specifications given for the crystal malt. For most recipes pale crystal malt is very suitable. Most Belgian beers are rather light amber anyway. In the darker versions, such as a Double, you can use a darker crystal malt. By now you probably understand that the color within a style can vary tremendously.

Preparing crystal malt is basically the same for each recipe. Add the required quantity of crushed crystal malt to one quart of water and bring to near boil. As soon as it is about to boil, stop and do not boil. Just strain immediately and add the liquid to the main brew.

Some recipes call for partial mash. To do this effectively, use one quart of water per one pound of ground malt (1 L/500 g). The water should be hot—preferably between 160 to 163 degrees F (71 to 73 degrees C). Just add the grain and mix thoroughly. You should have an equilibrium temperature of between 150 to 155 degrees F (65 to 68 degrees C).

In some recipes whole flour is also mentioned. As soon as all your malt is well hydrated, just use a household flour sifter to sift the flour over the mash. Then mix well enough to eliminate any lumps, and proceed as with a malt mash. Another way is to sift the flour over the water that you use for the mash. Mix thoroughly and use the milky fluid for mashing in. Leave there to mash 90 minutes. Check with the iodine to make sure that the saccharification is completed and then slowly raise the temperature to 170 degrees F (77 degrees C). This stops the enzymatic activity and gives the best viscosity for easy wort runoff.

Once the mash is completed, there are two different ways of proceeding according to recipes. In beers with a starting gravity below 1.055 sparge with one and one-half quarts (1.5 L) of water at 170 degrees F (77 degrees C). Sparge slowly until you collect two quarts of wort. In high gravity beers do not sparge. Just use the wort that seeps naturally from the grain. This ensures that you have more of the malt flavor without diluting it. It will be diluted anyway in the whole brew. In both cases, you just add the collected runoff to the whole batch.

Make sure that you boil for at least one and one-half hours. In recipes where you want a darker color you can boil longer. I have on occasion boiled wort for ninety minutes and then left it overnight just simmering at a temperature just below boiling with the cover on the brew pot. The next day I add finishing hops and cool the wort. It acquires a nice reddish, garnet color.

OUD BRUIN VRUCHT

Amount	5 gallons (Grain)	5 gallons (Extract)	1 barrel (Grain)
Pale malt:	8 lbs. (3.6 kg)	—	44 lbs. (20 kg)
Crystal malt:	2 oz. (57 g)	2 oz. (57 g)	11 oz. (308 g)
Pale dry extract:	—	5 lbs. (2.25 kg)	—
Color °L:	15° L	15° L	15° L
Bittering hops			
Saaz (4% alpha)	1 oz. (30 g)	1 oz. (30 g)	6 oz. (180 g)
HBU:	4	4	24
IBU:	20	20	20

Aroma hops			
Hallertauer			
(5% alpha)	0.5 oz. (15 g)	0.5 oz. (15 g)	3.2 oz. (96 g)

Fruits: 6 to 10 lbs. (2.7 kg - 4.5 kg) sour cherries or raspberry in secondary fermentation (for five gallons)

Water: soft water

Mash temperature: 151° - 153° F (66.1° - 67.2° C)

Original gravity: 1.048 (12° P)

Finishing gravity: 1.010 (2.5° P)

Priming sugar: 3 oz. (85 g) dextrose dissolved in 5 gallons

CO_2 (volumes): 2

Packaging: In bottles or draught

Note: In the malt extract brew, add crystal malt to one quart of water and bring it to boil. Strain the grains and add to the brew kettle. To achieve the right coloring, boil this for at least two hours; simmering overnight will deepen the color and give an orange-reddish tint. Leave fruits in secondary fermenter for at least three weeks. If you do not skimp on the fruit you are rewarded with a dry full-bodied, thirst-quenching, summer delight.

OUD BRUIN

Amount	5 gallons (Grain)	5 gallons (Extract)	1 barrel (Grain)
Pale malt:	7 lbs. (3.2 kg)	1 lb. (450 g)	38.5 lbs. (17.5 kg)
Crystal malt:	2 oz. (56 g)	2 oz. (56 g)	11 oz. (308 g)
Oat flour:	4 oz. (112 g)	4 oz. (112 g)	22 oz. (625 g)
Wheat flour:	4 oz. (112 g)	4 oz. (112 g)	22 oz. (625 g)
Amber malt syrup:	—	5 lbs. (2.25 kg)	—
Color °L:	15° L	15° L	15° L

Bittering hops			
Hallertauer			
(alpha 5%)	1.5 oz. (42 g)	1.5 oz. (42 g)	9 oz. (250 g)
HBU:	7.5	7.5	45
IBU:	22	22	22
Aroma hops			
Saaz (5% alpha)	0.3 oz. (10 g)	0.3 oz. (10 g)	1.8 oz. (60 g)

Water:	soft water
Mash temperature:	150° - 151° F (65.6° - 66.1° C)
Original gravity:	1.048 (12° P)
Finishing gravity:	1.008 - 0.010 (2° - 2.5° P)
Priming sugar:	3 oz. (85 g) dextrose dissolved in 5 gallons
CO_2 (volumes):	2 - 2.5
Packaging:	bottle

Note: Sift flours over mash and mix thoroughly. Extract brewers can follow grain directions in Saison recipe. To get proper coloring, boil at least two hours; simmering overnight will achieve a nice reddish color. Initial gravity should be around 1.042 (10.5° Plato).

Expect anything from this! Any yeast you use in this recipe puts you in the ballpark. Reddish color is obtained with the long boil or simmer.

SAISON

Amount	5 gallons (Grain)	5 gallons (Extract)	1 barrel (Grain)
Pale malt:	7.6 lbs. (3.4 kg)	0.5 lb. (454 g)	42 lbs. (19 kg)
Crystal malt:	3 oz. (85 g)	3 oz. (85 g)	17 oz. (510 g)
Chocolate malt:	0.3 oz. (10 g)	0.3 oz. (10 g)	1.8 oz. (60 g)
Wheat malt:	0.5 lb. (227 g)	0.5 lb. (454 g)	3 lbs. (2.75 kg)

Pale malt syrup:	—	3.3 lbs.	—
Pale dry extract:	—	2.25 lbs.	—
Sugar:	0.5 lb. (227 g)	0.5 lb. (454 g)	3 lbs. (2.75 kg)
Color °L:	10° L	10° L	10° L
Bittering hops			
Hallertauer			
(5% alpha)	1.5 oz. (42 g)	1.5 oz. (42 g)	9 oz. (252 g)
HBU:	7.5	7.5	45
IBU:	23	23	23
Aroma hops			
Saaz (4% alpha)	0.3 oz. (10 g)	0.3 oz. (10 g)	1.8 oz. (60 g)
Coriander	0.5 oz. (15 g)	0.5 oz. (15 g)	3 oz. (90 g)

Water:	soft water
Mash temperature:	149° - 150° F (65° - 66° C)
Original gravity:	1.054 (13.5° P)
Finishing gravity:	1.008 (2° P)
Priming sugar:	3 oz. (85 g) dextrose dissolved in 5 gallons
CO_2 (volumes):	2
Packaging:	bottle

Note: In the extract brew, add the wheat malt and the pale malt to three pints of water at 155 degrees F (65 degrees C) along with the crystal and chocolate malt. Hold for one hour, strain and sparge with two more quarts water. Coriander seeds (whole or ground) should be added to brew kettle at knock out.

Wheat malt gives a dry finish to this highly attenuated beer. Coriander is apparent in the aroma for about two months, then it disappears into a new aroma.

FLEMISH ALE

Amount	5 gallons (Grain)	5 gallons (Extract)	1 barrel (Grain)
Pale malt:	8 lbs. (3.6 kg)	—	44 lbs. (20 kg)
Crystal malt:	2 oz. (57 g)	2 oz. (57 g)	11 oz. (308 g)
Pale malt syrup:	—	6 lbs. (2.7 kg)	—
Pale dry extract:	—	—	—
Sugar:	—	—	—
Color °L:	8° L	8° L	8° L
Bittering hops			
Saaz (4% alpha)	1 oz. (30 g)	1 oz. (30 g)	6 oz. (180 g)
HBU:	4	4	24
IBU:	20	20	20
Aroma hops			
Goldings (5% alpha)	0.5 oz. (15 g)	0.5 oz. (15 g)	3.2 oz. (96 g)

Water:	soft water
Mash temperature:	151° - 153° F (66.1° - 67.2° C)
Original gravity:	1.048 (12° P)
Finishing gravity:	1.010 (2.5° P)
Priming sugar:	3 oz. (85 g) dextrose dissolved in 5 gallons
CO_2 (volumes):	2
Packaging:	bottle or draught

Note: In the malt extract brew, add the crystal malt to one quart of water and bring to a boil. Strain out the grains and add liquid to brew kettle.

A full gravity ale. With proper yeast, fruity aroma and body should be well complemented with the combination of Saaz and Goldings hops. This maintains the proper level of low hopped ales.

ST. HUMULUS - ABDIJ BIER

Amount	5 gallons (Grain)	5 gallons (Extract)	1 barrel (Grain)
Pale malt:	8 lbs. (3.6 kg)	—	44 lbs. (20 kg)
Munich malt:	3 lbs. (1.36 kg)	3 lbs. (1.36 g)	16.5 lbs. (7.5 kg)
Crystal malt:	4 oz. (112 g)	4 oz. (112 g)	22 oz. (615 g)
Pale malt syrup:	—	6 lbs. (2.7 kg)	—
Pale dry extract:	—	1 lb. (454 g)	—
Sugar:	1 lb. (454 g)	1 lb. (454 g)	6 lbs. (2.75 kg)
Color °L:	10 - 12° L	10 - 12° L	10 - 12° L
Bittering hops			
Perle (9% alpha)	1.2 oz. (34 g)	1.2 oz. (34 g)	7.2 oz. (200 g)
HBU:	10.8	10.8	64.8
IBU:	30	30	30
Aroma hops			
Goldings (5% alpha)	0.6 oz. (20 g)	0.6 oz. (20 g)	3.6 oz. (120 g)
Dry Hop: Saaz 5%:	0.3 oz. (10 g)	0.3 oz. (10 g)	1.8 oz (60 g)

Water:	soft water, but can be slightly hard
Mash temperature:	151° - 153° F (66.1° - 67.2° C)
Original gravity:	1.077 (19.25° P)
Finishing gravity:	1.014 (3.5° P)
Priming sugar:	3 oz. (85 g) dextrose dissolved in 5 gallons
CO_2 (volumes):	2 - 2.5
Packaging:	bottle

Note: In extract recipe, mix Munich malt with 4 quarts at 155 degrees F (68 degrees C) and hold for one hour. Sparge with 6 quarts of 170 degrees F (77degrees C) water, and add liquid to main brew.

The combination of Goldings and Saaz aroma with the lingering bitterness of Perle accentuates the lively body of the Munich and crystal malts, but without the dryness usually present in high-mineral-content water recommended for hoppy beers.

DOUBLE (DUBBEL)

Amount	5 gallons (Grain)	5 gallons (Extract)	1 barrel (Grain)
Pale malt:	9.5 lbs. (4.1 kg)	—	52 lbs. (22.5 kg)
Crystal malt:	4 oz. (112 g)	4 oz. (112 g)	24 oz. (672 g)
Brown malt:	4 oz. (112 g)	4 oz. (112 g)	24 oz. (672 g)
Pale malt syrup:	—	6 lbs. (2.7 kg)	—
Pale dry extract:	—	1.5 lbs. (680 g)	—
Sugar:	0.75 lb. (340 g)	0.75 lb. (340 g)	4.5 lbs. (2 kg)
Color °L:	14° L	14° L	14° L
Bittering hops			
Styrian (5% alpha)	1 oz. (28 g)	1 oz. (28 g)	6 oz. (170 g)
Hallertauer	0.3 oz. (10 g)	0.3 oz. (10 g)	1.8 oz. (60 g)
HBU:	6.5	6.5	39
IBU:	22	22	22
Aroma hops			
Saaz (4% alpha)	0.3 oz. (10 g)	0.3 oz. (10 g)	1.8 oz. (60 g)

Water: soft water
Mash temperature: 150° - 152° F (65.6° - 66.7° C)
Original gravity: 1.065 (16.25° P)
Finishing gravity: 1.013 (3.25° P)

Priming sugar:	3 oz. (85 g) dextrose dissolved in 5 gallons
CO_2 (volumes):	2 - 2.5
Packaging:	bottle

Note: This is a good recipe to experiment with sugars. You could use corn sugar, glucose syrup, brown or raw sugar, demerara sugar or *candi* sugar (if available).

Malt aroma and body should be present in this one. The brown malt gives an increase in color but does not add a particular taste. This is a good one to enjoy a full taste in a beer where sugar is added. Use dark crystal malt.

TRIPPLE (TRIPPEL)

Amount	5 gallons (Grain)	5 gallons (Extract)	1 barrel (Grain)
Pale malt:	12 lbs. (5.4 kg)	—	66 lbs. (30 kg):
Pale malt syrup:	—	6 lbs. (2.7 kg)	—
Pale dry extract:	—	3 lbs. (1.36 kg)	—
Sugar:	1.5 lbs. (680 g)	1.5 lbs. (680 g)	9 lbs. (4 kg)
Color °L:	3.5° - 5° L	3.5° - 5° L	3.5° - 5° L
Bittering hops			
Hallertauer (5% alpha)	1.3 oz. (36 g)	1.3 oz. (36 g)	7.8 oz. (216 g)
Styrian (5% alpha)	0.3 oz. (10 g)	0.3 oz. (10 g)	1.8 oz. (60 g)
HBU:	8	8	48
IBU:	25	25	25
Aroma hops			
Saaz (4% alpha)	0.5 oz. (15 g)	0.5 oz. (15 g)	3 oz. (90 g)
Water:	soft water		

Mash temperature:	150° - 151° F (65.6° - 66.1° C)
Original gravity:	1.081 (20.25° P)
Finishing gravity:	1.012 (3° P)
Priming sugar:	3 oz. (85 g) dextrose dissolved in 5 gallons
CO_2 (volumes):	2 - 2.5
Packaging:	bottle

Note: In this recipe you must really use a light sugar such as dextrose or glucose syrup to get the genuine taste.

This should look almost like a Pils but with tons of taste. Not bitter, but refreshing. The alcohol taste should not be noticeable, but is felt in the aftertaste.

SANTA CLAUS' MAGIC POTION

Amount	5 gallons (Grain)	5 gallons (Extract)	1 barrel (Grain)
Pale malt:	12.5 lbs. (5.7 kg)	—	69 lb. (31.3 kg)
Crystal malt:	4 oz. (112 g)	4 oz. (112 g)	24 oz. (108 g)
Chocolate malt:	2 oz. (56 g)	2 oz. (56 g)	12 oz. (336 g)
Pale malt syrup:	—	6 lbs. (2.7 kg)	—
Pale dry extract:	—	3 lbs. (2.45 kg)	—
Sugar:	2 lbs. (900 g)	2 lbs. (900 g)	12 lbs. (5.4 kg)
Color °L:	12° - 14° L	12° - 14° L	12° - 14° L
Spices			
Sweet gale seeds:	0.03 oz. (1 g)	0.03 oz. (1 g)	0.18 oz. (6 g)
nutmeg:	0.03 oz. (1 g)	0.03 oz. (1 g)	0.18 oz. (6 g)
Bittering hops			
Perle (9% alpha)	1.5 oz. (42 g)	1.5 oz. (42 g)	9 oz. (250 g)
HBU:	13.5	13.5	81
IBU:	35	35	35

Aroma hops			
Tettnanger			
(4% alpha)	0.5 oz. (15 g)	0.5 oz. (15 g)	3 oz. (90 g)

Water:	soft water
Mash temperature:	151° - 153° F (66.1° - 67.2° C)
Original gravity:	1.090 (21.5° P)
Finishing gravity:	1.018 (4.6° P)
Priming sugar:	3 oz. (85 g) dextrose dissolved in 5 gallons
CO_2 (volumes):	2 - 2.5
Packaging:	bottle

Note: In the malt extract brew, the crystal malt and chocolate malt should be added to one quart of water and brought to boil. Strain the grains and add to brew kettle. This recipe comes out extremely well with a dark sugar. Dark *candi* is the best but demerara, dark raw or dark brown can be used instead. A mixture of one pound dark honey with one pound sugar works well also. Put spices in kettle at end of boil.

This is the kind of beer that you have only now and then, but each time the taste evolves. The major aromatic component is the sweet gale, with the nutmeg right behind.

CHOU-CHOU

Amount	**5 gallons (Grain)**	**5 gallons (Extract)**	**1 barrel (Grain)**
Pale malt:	13.2 lbs. (6 kg)	—	71.5 lb (32.5 kg)
Pale malt syrup:	—	6.6 lbs. (3 kg)	—
Pale dry extract:	—	3.3 lbs. (1.5 kg)	—
Sugar: dark candi:	6.5 oz. (180 g)	6.5 oz. (180 g)	2.2 lbs. (1 kg)
Color °L:	7° L	7° L	7° L

Bittering hops			
Styrian (5% alpha)	0.6 oz. (18 g)	0.6 oz. (18 g)	4 oz. (110 g)
HBU:	3	3	18
IBU:	18	18	18
Coriander seeds:	0.6 oz. (18 g)	0.5 oz. (18 g)	2 oz. (50 g)

Aroma hops			
Hersbruck (5% alpha):	0.3 oz. (9 g)	0.3 oz. (9 g)	2 oz. (55 g)
Hallertauer (5% alpha):	0.3 oz. (9 g)	0.3 oz. (9 g)	2 oz. (55 g)
Northern Moravia (3.8% alpha)	0.5 oz. (15 g)	0.5 oz. (15 g)	3 oz. (90 g)

Water:	soft water
Mash temperature:	(see note below)
Original gravity:	1.088 (22° P)
Finishing gravity:	1.022 (5.4° P)
Priming sugar:	3 oz. (85 g) dextrose dissolved in 5 gallons
CO_2 (volumes):	2 - 2.5
Packaging:	bottle

Note: In chapter 4, "Brewing with a Belgian Brewmaster" gives lots of pertinent details.

After two weeks in the bottle, this is already great. The combination of hops and coriander create a new aroma in which the distinct components are hard to detect. Lots of body but without an alcoholic taste.

DRIVER'S CHOICE (BIERE DE TABLE, LOW ALCOHOL)

Amount	5 gallons (Grain)	5 gallons (Extract)	1 barrel (Grain)
Pale malt:	2.5 lbs. (1.13 kg)	—	15 lbs. (6.75 kg)
Crystal malt:	4 oz. (112 g)	4 oz. (112 g)	24 oz. (675 g)
Pale dry extract:	—	1.75 lbs. (800 g)	—
100% dextrine			
Powder:	2 oz. (56 g)	2 oz. (56 g)	12 oz. (336 g)
Color °L:	3.5° - 5.5° L	3.5° - 5.5° L	3.5° - 5.5° L
Bittering hops			
Hallertauer			
(5% alpha)	0.6 oz. (20 g)	0.6 oz. (20 g)	3.6 oz. (120 g)
HBU:	3	3	18
IBU:	12	12	12
Aroma hops			
Saaz (4% alpha)	0.3 oz. (10 g)	0.3 oz. (10 g)	1.8 oz. (60 g)

Water: soft water
Mash temperature: 149° - 150° F (65° - 66° C)
Original gravity: 1.016 (4° P)
Finishing gravity: 1.006 - 8 (1.5° - 4° P)
Priming sugar: 3 oz. (85 g) dextrose dissolved in 5 gallons
CO_2 (volumes): 2 - 2.5
Packaging: bottle

Note: This low alcohol beer should be drunk quickly. Most people never think of making a low alcohol beer.

Although this does not taste like your regular brew the combination of hops and crystal malt is refreshing and still fulfilling.

GOUDEN CHARLIE

Amount	5 gallons (Grain)	5 gallons (Extract)	1 barrel (Grain)
Pale malt:	5.5 lbs. (2.5 kg)	—	30 lbs. (13.75 kg)
Munich malt:	5 lbs. (2.3 kg)	—	27.5 lbs. (12.5 g)
Pale malt syrup:	—	6.6 lbs. (3 kg)	—
Amber dry extract:	—	1 lb. (454 g)	—
Orange blossom			—
honey:	1 lb. (454 g)	1 lb. (454 g)	6 lbs. (2.7 kg)
Color °L:	12° L	12° L	12° L
Bittering hops			
Golding (5% alpha)	1.2 oz. (33 g)	1.2 oz. (33 g)	7.2 oz. (200 g)
Tettnanger (4% alpha)	0.8 oz. (20 g)	0.8 oz. (20 g)	4.8 oz. (120 g)
HBU:	9.2	9.2	55.2
IBU:	25	25	25
Aroma hops			
Tettnanger (4% alpha)	0.3 oz. (10 g)	0.3 oz. (10 g)	1.8 oz. (60 g)

Water:	soft water
Mash temperature:	151° - 153° F (66.1° - 67.2° C)
Original gravity:	1.070 (17.5° P)
Finishing gravity:	1.014 (3.5° P)
Priming sugar:	3 oz. (85 g) dextrose dissolved in 5 gallons
CO_2 (volumes):	2 - 2.5
Packaging:	bottle

Note: If unable to find orange blossom honey, any other type can do, but add into brew kettle at knock out 0.3 oz. (10 g) of dried bitter orange peel to get similar taste and aroma.

The combination of Munich malt with orange blossom honey creates a totally new sustained and animated mouthfeel. This is a good one to follow in taste evolution.

SILK LADY

Amount	5 gallons (Grain)	5 gallons (Extract)	1 barrel (Grain)
Pale malt:	4 lbs. (1.8 kg)	1.5 lbs. (0.7 kg)	22 lbs. (9.9 kg)
Wheat malt:	3.5 lbs. (1.6 kg)	1 lb. (.5 kg)	19.25 lbs.(8.75 kg)
Pale dry extract:	—	2 lbs. (1 kg)	—
Wheat malt syrup:	—	2 lbs. (1 kg)	—
Whole wheat flour:	0.5 lb. (.25 kg)	2.5 oz. (70 g)	2.75 lbs.(1.25 kg)
Color °L:	3 - 5° L	3 - 5° L	3 - 5° L
Bittering hops			
Saaz (4% alpha)	1 oz. (30 g)	1 oz. (30 g)	6 oz. (180 g)
HBU:	4	4	24
IBU:	20	20	20
Aroma hops			
Saaz (4% alpha)	0.5 oz. (15 g)	0.5 oz. (15 g)	6 oz. (180 g)
Coriander seeds	0.5 oz. (15 g)	0.5 oz. (15 g)	3 oz. (90 g)
Fresh ground ginger:	0.1 oz. (3 g)	0.1 oz. (3 g)	0.1 oz. (3 g)

Water:	soft water
Mash temperature:	151° - 153° F (66.1° - 67.2° C)
Original gravity:	1.048 (12° P)

Finishing gravity:	1.010 (2.5° P)
Priming sugar:	3 oz. (85 g) dextrose dissolved in 5 gallons
CO_2 (volumes):	2
Packaging:	bottles or draught

Note: Add coriander seeds (whole or ground) to the brew kettle at knock out. Flour should be sifted over mash and mixed thoroughly. Extract brewers can follow grain directions in *Saison* recipe.

The combination of coriander and ginger along with the whitish color of the beer makes others wonder what you have used. Follow the aroma evolution of this one. It keeps moving along.

SIERRA BLANCA

Amount	5 gallons (Grain)	5 gallons (Extract)	1 barrel (Grain)
Pale malt:	4 lbs. (1.8 kg)	—	22 lbs. (9.9 kg)
Wheat malt:	4 lbs. (1.8 kg)	—	22 lbs. (9.9 kg)
Pale malt syrup:	—	3 lbs. (1.3 kg)	—
Wheat malt syrup:	—	3 lbs. (1.3 kg)	—
Sugar	—	—	—
Color °L:	3 - 5° L	3 - 5° L	3 - 5° L
Bittering hops			
Saaz (4% alpha)	1 oz. (30 g)	1 oz. (30 g)	6 oz. (180 g)
HBU:	4	4	24
IBU:	20	20	20
Aroma hops			
Saaz (4% alpha)	0.5 oz. (15 g)	0.5 oz. (15 g)	3.2 oz. (96 g)
Coriander seeds:	0.75 oz. (20 g)	0.75 oz. (20 g)	4.5 oz. (125 g)
Dried orange peel:	0.2 oz. (5 g)	0.2 oz. (5 g)	1.2 oz. (30 g)

Water:	soft water
Mash temperature:	151° - 153° F (66.1° - 67.2° C)
Original gravity:	1.048 (12° P)
Finishing gravity:	1.010 (2.5° P)
Priming sugar:	3 oz. (85 g) dextrose dissolved in 5 gallons
CO_2 (volumes):	2
Packaging:	bottles or draught

Note: Add coriander seeds (whole or ground) and dried bitter orange peels to the brew kettle at knock out.

The taste of this one can vary a lot depending on the yeast used. Acidic aftertaste combined with the powerful aroma contrasts with the sustained vigorous body.

GRAND CRU

Amount	5 gallons (Grain)	5 gallons (Extract)	1 barrel (Grain)
Pale malt:	9 lbs. (4 kg)	—	49 lbs. (22 kg)
Crystal malt:	4 oz. (110 g)	4 oz. (110 g)	24 oz. (675 g)
Chocolate malt:	0.3 oz. (10 g)	0.3 oz. (10 g)	1.8 oz. (60 g)
Pale malt syrup:	—	3.3 lbs. (1.5 kg)	—
Pale dry extract:	—	3.5 lbs. (1.6 kg)	—
Sugar:	1 lb. (450 g)	1 lb. (450g)	6 lb. (2.7 kg)
Color °L:	10 - 12° L	10 - 12° L	10 - 12° L
Bittering hops			
Styrian (5% alpha)	1.5 oz. (42 g)	1.5 oz. (42 g)	9 oz. (252 g)
HBU:	7.5	7.5	45
IBU:	23	23	23
Aroma hops			
Golding (5% alpha)	0.6 oz. (20 g)	0.6 oz. (20 g)	3.6 oz. (120 g)

Water:	soft water
Mash temperature:	152° - 154° F (66.7° - 76.8° C)
Original gravity:	1.063 (15.75° P)
Finishing gravity:	1.012 - 1.015 (3°-3.75° P)
Priming sugar:	3 oz. (85 g) dextrose dissolved in 5 gallons
CO_2 (volumes):	2 - 2.5
Packaging:	bottle

Note: This recipe is great for two-yeast fermentation. First fermentation takes place with a weak attenuating yeast. In the secondary fermenter, add a second wild type, or different higher attenuating yeast. Even with one yeast this works very well.

Each brewer has a different version of this one. The hop should come out nicely with the malt, but with little bitterness.

Appendix A: Commercial Examples

Selecting examples of a style from over 600 brand names is a difficult task. I have selected examples of commercial beers that, first, can most likely can be found and, second, that truly represent the majority of the beers within the category. However, interesting variants are also mentioned with the hope that you try to find them and broaden your scope of knowledge and taste.

On occasions I have tasted these beers with North American brewers (both amateurs and professionals) and have found them disoriented and perplexed by the novel and original tastes and aromas. Comments like, "What, no hops?" or "Infected!" are quite common. The trend in North America has been to judge and comment on a beer by the presence or absence of defects, and not by the abundance and originality of its qualities. We must remember that these beers are brewed by professionals educated in the field of brewing science to fulfill the requirements of their customers. Long traditions and acceptance has maintained loyal followings in what are perceived as strange tastes to North Americans. Also, most of these beer are in the category of "met smaakevolutie - au gout évolutif" — "taste changes with time." Samples tasted in North America can be quite different than samples tasted in Belgium because of age, handling or mishandling.

TRAPPIST BEER

The Trappist beers vary so much within their classification that we must mention them all.

Orval—A truly unique beer. The Trappist beer with the lowest alcohol content: 4.2 percent w/v or 5.2 percent v/v. Apricot gold, powerful unique aroma combining hops, yeasts, and malt. One of the most bitter beers in the world. Dry-hopped for one month. Effervescent like Champagne, with powerful taste and long bitter aftertaste. The kind of beer that you either hate or love.

Chimay—The biggest producer with at least three beers. Main characteristic is powerful estery nose as a result of high temperature fermentation. Big malty body with medium bitterness, except the white, which has a long, dry, bitter, almost acidic aftertaste.

Westmalle—Originator of the Tripel. Looks like a Pils. Subdued malt and hop aroma. Big, dry-on-the-malty-side taste with clean short aftertaste. Clean, refreshing and sustained taste.

Westvletteren—Available only at the monastery and a few specialty stores. The 12° Abt is regarded as their finest example. Big malty and estery nose. Rich sustained body mildly alcoholic with average effervescence. Mellow aftertaste. I once drank a ten-year-old sample of this beer and it was something that I could never have imagined. The effervescence was almost gone and it tasted like a rich port, with nuances of raisins, hazelnuts, malt, and liqueur. It's hard to believe that this is a beer! Brewed also under license by a commercial brewer, under the name of St. Sixtus.

Rochefort—They brew the strongest Trappist beer on the market. The Rochefort 10 packs a whopping alcohol content (9 percent w/v or 11.2 percent v/v). Big estery nose with mild chocolate undertones. Young samples can have an alcoholic taste. The body is on the light side and the aftertaste on the sweetish side. Let it age.

ABBEY (ABDIJ) BEER

Maredsous—Brewed by Moortgat the brewer of Duvel. They have a 6°, 8°, 9° and a 10°L. The 6°L is probably the best. Big full body and pleasant aromatic nose. Being only 4.8 percent w/v (6 percent v/v) you can enjoy two instead of one.

Cuvée de l'Ermitage—Brewed by Brasserie Union and sold in 250 ml bottle. This is the most Pale-Ale-like abbey beer. Big hoppy nose combined with subdued malt aroma. Rich sustained body soon replaced by long smooth lingering bitterness. This beer is filtered and pasteurized.

St. Idesbald Abdij—A unique tasting beer, in a class with Orval. Aroma of Lambic and Oud Bruin. Feels in the mouth like you have ten different beers one after the other. A quick succession of different tastes from sour to malty and acidic, all wrapped up in immense sustained body. A quick succession of aftertastes and it's all gone without a trace, just a pleasant souvenir. The brown has a shade more body than the pale. A well-kept secret.

Leffe Radieuse—High-tech abbey beer brewed by the Artois, the Mt. St. Guibert subsidiary of Interbrew. Big clean aromatic nose, smooth rounded body and long clean finish. A superb example of a high alcohol beer that has no alcohol taste. If Anheuser-Busch ever brews an abbey beer this is what they have to beat.

TRIPPLE (TRIPPEL)

Affligem—A triple with a tremendously rich aromatic nose. A combination of esters and malt complemented by hops that you can't detect but you know are there. Rich, sustained, and lively body fills the mouth instantly. Velvety smooth in the aftertaste. This and Westmalle (a Trappist beer) are truly outstanding examples of Triples.

Grimbergen—Brewed by Brasserie Union, a subsidiary of Alken Maes. An easy-drinking Triple. A favorite of those who like a beer with subdued aroma and taste. A good starting point to acquaint yourself with Triples.

Augustin—This is another Triple with a big malty estery nose. Rich rounded body. Delicate, dry, subdued finish without hop bitterness.

Corsendonk Agnus—This is a triple with a noticeable coriander nose in young samples. This aroma disappears with age to create an "I-don't-know what-it-is" new aroma.

Brugse Trippel—Another excellent example of the style. This is a strong triple (7.6 percent w/v or 9.5 percent v/v) and has such a good equilibrium that you can't detect the taste of alcohol, just feel its warmth.

DOUBLE (DUBBEL)

Westmalle Double—Technically this is a Trappist beer. This double could be called the standard for the class. An immense, complex nose with a predominance of ester from fermentation. Fruity palate, generous body, and a slightly bigger aftertaste. One you can't forget.

Grimbergen—This is a good commercial example of a double and is relatively easy to find. Nice aromatic nose, with a mildly malty mouthfeel and a short finish on the dry side. Filtered and pasteurized.

Bornem Double—This is an example of the style with a subdued nose and aroma. Light tasting and drinkable. The malt and estery aroma is light. The body has a rich neutral taste with a dry, subdued aftertaste.

SPECIAL

Duvel—The most popular special sold in Belgium. A few years ago it had a distinct aroma and character that made it unique. Recent samples have not shown as much personality. The aroma is neutral with a hint of fruitiness; the body is still immense but with a neutral taste and a quick, dry finish. Probably a victim of success.

La Chouffe—A special with a unique spicy character. This is the kind of beer that really has a character that develops by stages. Young samples have a hint of coriander in the nose. After a few weeks it gets spicy. You smell a uniqueness from the yeast. The palate is a mixture of malt and spices. The finish is dry with a touch of sweetness.

Oerbier—This is a typical hoppy beer, Belgian style. The nose is a combination of malt esters, hops, and chocolate. The palate is fruity and the mouthfeel rich and sustained. You taste the hops but with little bitterness. A lingering aftertaste goes down in stages from sweet to dry and then a final subtle hop bitterness.

Delirium Tremens—This is a beer that the brewer has

chosen to name a special but it could be a triple. You need a good glass to retain the foam on this one. Hints of vanilla in the nose. Big body with a rich mouthfeel. Long, sweet aftertaste.

Lucifer—Here again a beer that is almost a triple. Young samples have a neutral nose, but acquire a nice malty-estery character with age. The palate also improves with age. Finish is mostly dry but with a touch of sweetness.

Arcen Grand Prestige—This is the kind of beer that has no business in a book about Belgian beer because it is made in Holland. But because nobody is going to write a book about beers from Holland and because it is brewed a few miles from Belgium in a typical Belgian style I cannot ignore what I consider a superb example of a special. The nose on this is a unique combination originating from the yeast strain. It is estery-malty with an addition of woodsy undertone similar to the aroma of old wooden casks. Subtle palate with many taste levels. Malty, fruity, woodsy almost liquor-like taste. Long aftertaste that goes down in steps to a final dry finish. A unique beer.

Gauloise—A dark amber speciality beer with a dash of coriander aroma. This is a typical example of coloring obtained from dark candi sugar. No specialty malt taste but a deep color. Rich body balanced with a high alcohol content (7.2 percent w/v or 9 percent v/v). Nice finish with a subdued sweetness.

Gouden Carolus—Dark amber beer with a reddish tint. Aroma of figs and raisins. Hints of woodsiness in the palate with animated currents of liquor—like aged beer. Strong but mild. The alcohol is noticeable only from its warmth. The aftertaste lingers with an underlying slight bitterness.

ALES AND SAISON

De Koninck—Once you have had a De Koninck on draught you understand why this is the most popular beer in Antwerp. There is served in a glass that implies invitation to a religious ceremony. The head on the glass is more impressive (and real) than in beer commercials. The aroma is fruity and inviting. The palate is mellow, fruity and accentuated with just a hint of hops. The aftertaste is subdued and disappears like a thief in the night. In the bottle—forget it.

Vieux temps—An ale brewed by the Mt. St. Guibert subsidiary of Interbrew. Technically perfect without defects, but also without a great personality. A nice subtle aroma, a remarkable body and an individual taste from the yeast. Easily available on draught.

Special Palm—Another beer with a large distribution. One of the best buys in the bottle. Nice fruity aroma and palate. Distinctive taste.

Artevelde Grand Cru—Brewed by Huyghe in Melle to comply with the Reinheitsgebot. This medium-alcohol (4.5 percent w/v or 5.6 percent v/v) ale is refermented in the bottle. The many perfumes present in the nose denote instantly that special yeasts are at work in this one. The aroma of old casks is present. The mouthfeel brings you to many places. Malty, sweet, and hoppy accents are here set against tastes of old wooden kegs. Long sustained aftertaste brings you down gently. A relatively low alcohol level allows you to have a second.

Saison Regal—This is the Saison that is most widely available. It is light amber. A slight coriander nose in young samples fades rapidly in a few weeks. It has what some people call a musty aroma. The effervescence is medium. The taste is rather neutral and the finish light and dry.

Saison Silly—A nice fruity aroma. The palate is full and mellow with a hint of acidity. The aftertase is appropriately neutral and on the dry side.

WHITE BEER

Hoegaardse Wit—This is the one that started the comeback after white beer had all but disappeared. Typical acidic and fruity aroma. A dash of coriander and orange in the nose complements the typical aroma conferred by the wheat. Fruity palate explodes in the mouth with its effervescence. Nice, dry, slightly acidic finish. At its best on draft.

Dentergem Wit—Similar to Hoegaardse but the body has a little more "meat" and "chewiness." Here again, great on draft.

Blanke Wit—This is a pleasant one with a generous acidity level. Aroma is not fruity as others, but it's a real thirst quencher.

Blanche des Neiges—This relative newcomer on the white beer scene has a generous homemade nose that is different from the others. It's combination of spices creates a unique aroma in which you cannot detect the individual components. This unique blend is noticeable in the taste and balanced with the body. Long dry aftertaste is not as acidic as others. This beer is refermented in the bottle and pasteurized.

OUD BRUIN

Leifmans Goudenband—This is a great example of a patiently hand-crafted beer. Generous aroma combines the tastes of acidic, fruity and malt. Undertones of woods and wines. Generous body with a rich palette of tastes. Starts softly and then the carbonation develops a slight sensation of spiciness followed by a lively acidic tang. Keeps forever, but keep your bottles lying down on their side.

Felix Speciaal Oudenaarde—Another good example of Oud Bruin. Its nose is very fruity and predominates. This is a well-rounded, easy-drinking, slightly sour and acidic beer. The aftertaste is short and pleasantly refreshing.

Rodenbach—This is the most widely available beer of the style. Many places have it on draft. Well balanced, fruity nose. Good vinous taste combines well with the sour and acid. Its almost reddish color leads you to believe you are drinking wine.

Appendix B: Reading Belgian Beer Labels

The label on a Belgian beer found in North America is at times lacking information. Marketing specialists make sure that not much is said to inform the consumer except what is required or fobidden by various state and provincial laws. However if you get to Belgium and want to purchase beer, you are more than likely faced with a label written in Flemish, French or Italian. So here are a few phrases from labels of various beers with an explanation of their meaning.

(1) Hoge gisting met nagisting in de fles
Fermentation haute refermentée en bouteille

This means that it's a top-fermented ale and the beer has been refermented in the bottle.

(2) Bier op gist
Bière sur lie

Refermented in the bottle

(3) Levend bier
Bière vivante

Literally, a beer that's "alive," with yeast in the bottle and unlikely to be pasteurized.

(4) Fris opdienen
Servir frais

Serve cooled (but never under 45 degrees F [7 degrees C]).

(5) Ten minste houdbaar tot einde
A consommer de préféference avant fin:

Best before: (Although this phrase is on many labels, the date seldom is.)

(6) Gebotteld Datum:
Embouteillé le:

Bottling date

(7) Met smaakevolutie
Au gout évolutif

This tells you that the taste of this beer will change in time. Usually this is the best sign of quality. These beers are refermented in the bottle and seldom pasteurized.

(8) Gebrouwt enkel met water, mout, kandij, hop, gist. Niet gefiltered - niet gepasteuriseerd

Brassé seulement avec de l'eau, du malt, sucre candi, houblons et levure. Non filtrée - non pasteurisée.

Brewed only with water, malt, candi sugar, hops and yeast. Not filtered and not pasteurized. This notice is a sign of quality.

(9) Ambachtelijk bier driemaal gegist
Biére artisanale a triple fermentation

Handcrafted beer that has had three fermentations.

(10) Echt Oudenaards oud bruin bier van hoge gisting, artisanaal gebrouwen.

Vieille brune d'Audenarde de fermentation haute brassée artisanalement.

Old Oudernaards brown ale, handcrafted.

(11) Wit beer, op traditionele wijze naar oud Vlaams recept gebrouwen, uit tarwe, haver, gerstemout, licht gearomatiseerd met natuurlijke kruiden.

Bière blanche brassée artisanalement, de froment, avoine, malt, suivant une ancienne recette Flamande, aromatisée avec des herbes naturelles.

White beer, handcrafted according to an old Flemish recipe, with wheat, oats, and malt. Flavored with natural herbs.

(12) De houdbaarheid van dit bier is onbegrensd
La qualité de cette biére se maintient indefiniment

Literally: "This beer is good forever." Usually true.

Appendix C: Belgian Brewing Schools

To most brewers in North America the only place in the world where there are brewing schools is in Germany. However it may surprise you that in Belgium there are at least five places where you can learn brewing science and earn either a brewmaster diploma or brewing engineer diploma. Quite often the courses are given simultaneously in French and Flemish. Fundamental fermentation and brewing research is undertaken in these schools and studies up to the doctorate level are offered.

Following is an alphabetical list of these institutions, in an order that indicates no preference.

Hogere School Voor Gistingsbedrijven C.T.L. - Gent

Institut des industries de fermentation de Bruxelles. CERIA (Instituut voor Gistingsbedrijven te Brussel - COOVI)

Katholieke Industriele Hogeschool Oost - Vlaanderen St.-Lievens-Gent

Katholieke Universiteit - Leuven

Université de Louvain-La-Neuve
Sciences et Technologies Brassicoles

Information on these schools and on Belgian beers can be obtained by writing to the association of Belgian breweries:

Confédération des Brasseurs de Belgique
Confederate der Brouwerijn van Belgie
Maison des Brasseurs
Grote Markt 10
Brussels
Belgium

Glossary

adjunct. Any *unmalted* grain or other fermentable ingredient added to the mash.

aeration. The action of introducing air to the wort at various stages of the brewing process.

airlock. (see fermentation lock)

airspace. (see ullage)

alcohol by volume (v/v). The percentage of volume of alcohol per volume of beer. To calculate the approximate volumetric alcohol content, subtract the terminal gravity from the original gravity and divide the result by 7.5. For example: 1050 - 1012 = 38 / 7.5 = 5% v/v.

alcohol by weight (w/v). The percentage weight of alcohol per volume of beer. For example: 3.2% alcohol by weight = 3.2 grams of alcohol per 100 centiliters of beer.

ale. 1. Historically, an unhopped malt beverage. 2. Now a generic term for hopped beers produced by top fermentation, as opposed to lagers, which are produced by bottom fermentation.

all-extract beer. A beer made with only malt extract as opposed to one made from barley, or a combination of malt extract and barley.

all-grain beer. A beer made with only malted barley as opposed to one made from malt extract, or from malt extract and malted barley.

all-malt beer. A beer made with only barley malt with no adjuncts or refined sugars.

alpha acid. A soft resin in hop cones. When boiled, alpha acids are converted to iso-alpha-acids, which account for 60 percent of a beer's bitterness.

alpha-acid unit. A measurement of the potential bitterness of hops, expressed by their percentage of alpha acid. Low = 2 to 4%, medium = 5 to 7%, high = 8 to 12%. Abbrev: A.A.U.

attenuation. The reduction in the wort's specific gravity caused by the transformation of sugars into alcohol and carbon-dioxide gas.

Balling. A saccharometer invented by Carl Joseph Napoleon Balling in 1843. It is calibrated for 63.5 degrees F (17.5 degrees C), and graduated in grams per hundred, giving a direct reading of the percentage of extract by weight per 100 grams solution. For example: 10 °B = 10 grams of sugar per 100 grams of wort.

blow-by (blow-off). A single-stage homebrewing fermentation method in which a plastic tube is fitted into the mouth of a carboy, with the other end submerged in a pail of sterile water. Unwanted residues and carbon dioxide are expelled through the tube, while air is prevented from coming into contact with the fermenting beer, thus avoiding contamination.

carbonation. The process of introducing carbon-dioxide gas into a liquid by: 1. injecting the finished beer with carbon dioxide; 2. adding young fermenting beer to finished beer for a renewed fermentation (kraeusening); 3. priming (adding sugar) to fermented wort prior to bottling, creating a secondary fermentation in the bottle.

carboy. A large glass, plastic or earthenware bottle.

chill haze. Haziness caused by protein and tannin during the secondary fermentation.

dry hopping. The addition of hops to the primary fermenter, the secondary fermenter, or to casked beer to add aroma and hop character to the finished beer without adding significant bitterness.

dry malt. Malt extract in powdered form.

extract. The amount of dissolved materials in the wort after mashing and lautering malted barley and/or malt adjuncts such as corn and rice.

fermentation lock. A simple device that allows carbon-dioxide gas to escape from the fermenter while excluding contaminants.

final specific gravity. The specific gravity of a beer when fermentation is complete.

fining. The process of adding clarifying agents to beer during secondary fermentation to precipitate suspended matter.

flocculation. The behavior of yeast cells joining into masses and settling out toward the end of fermentation.

homebrew bittering units. A formula invented by the American Homebrewers Association to measure bitterness valve of beer. Example: 1.5 ounces of hops at 10 percent alpha acid for five gallons: 1.5 x 10 = 15 HBU per five gallons.

hop pellets. Finely powdered hop cones compressed into tablets. Hop pellets are 20 to 30 percent more bitter by weight than the same variety in loose form.

hydrolysis. A chemical reaction in which a compound reacts with the ions of water (H+ or OH-) to produce a weak acid, a weak base or both.

hydrometer. A glass instrument used to measure the specific gravity of liquids as compared to water, consisting of a graduated stem resting on a weighted float.

International bitterness units. This is an empirical quantity which was originally designed to measure the concentration of iso-alpha-acids in milligrams per liter (parts per million). Most procedures will also measure a small amount of uncharacterized soft resins so IBUs are generally 5 to 10% higher than iso-alpha acid concentrations. Also referred to simply as "Bittering Units."

isinglass. A gelatinous substance made from the swim bladder of certain fish and added to beer as a fining agent.

kraeusen. (n.) The rocky head of foam which appears on the surface of the wort during fermentation. (v.) To add fermenting wort to fermented beer to induce carbonation through a secondary fermentation.

lager. (n.) A generic term for any bottom-fermented beer. Lager brewing is now the predominant brewing method worldwide except in Britain where top fermented ales dominate. (v.) To store beer at near-zero temperatures in order to precipitate yeast cells and proteins and promote a "cleaner" taste.

lauter tun. A vessel in which the mash settles and the grains are removed from the sweet wort through a straining process. It has a false, slotted bottom and spigot.

liquefaction. The process by which alpha-amylase enzymes degrade soluble starch into dextrin.

malt. Barley that has been steeped in water, germinated, then dried in kilns. This process converts insoluble starchs to soluble substances and sugars.

malt extract. A thick syrup or dry powder prepared from malt.

mashing. Mixing ground malt with water to extract the fermentables, degrade haze-forming proteins and convert grain starches to fermentable sugars and nonfermentable carbohydrates.

modification. 1. The physical and chemical changes in barley as a result of malting. 2. The degree to which these changes have occured, as determined by the growth of the acrospire.

original gravity. The specific gravity of wort previous to fermentation. A measure of the total amount of dissolved solids in wort.

pH. A measure of acidity or alkalinity of a solution, usually on a scale of one to 14, where seven is neutral.

Plato. A saccharometer that expresses specific gravity as extract weight in a one-hundred-gram solution at 68 degrees F (20 degrees C). A revised, more accurate version of Balling, developed by Dr. Plato.

primary fermentation. The first stage of fermentation, during which most fermentable sugars are converted to ethyl alcohol and carbon dioxide.

priming sugar. A small amount of corn, malt or cane sugar added to bulk beer prior to racking or at bottling to induce a new fermentation and create carbonation.

racking. The process of transferring beer from one container to another, especially into the final package (bottles, kegs, etc.).

saccharification. The naturally occurring process in which malt starch is converted into fermentable sugars, primarily maltose.

saccharometer. An instrument that determines the sugar concentration of a solution by measuring the specific gravity.

secondary fermentation. 1. The second, slower stage of fermentation, lasting from a few weeks to many months depending on the type of beer. 2. A fermentation occuring in bottles or casks and initiated by priming or by adding yeast.

sparging. Spraying the spent grains in the mash with hot water to retrieve the remaining malt sugar.

specific gravity. A measure of a substance's density as compared to that of water, which is given the value of 1.000 at 39.2 degrees F (4 degrees C). Specific gravity has no accompanying units, because it is expressed as a ratio.

starter. A batch of fermenting yeast, added to the wort to initiate fermentation.

strike temperature. The initial temperature of the water when the malted barley is added to it to create the mash.

trub. Suspended particles resulting from the precipitation of proteins, hop oils and tannins during boiling and cooling stages of brewing.

ullage. The empty space between a liquid and the top of its container. Also called airspace or headspace.

v/v: (see alcohol by volume)

w/v: (see alcohol by weight)

water hardness. The degree of dissolved minerals in water.

wort. The mixture that results from mashing the malt and boiling the hops, before it is fermented into beer.

Index

Bibliography

Baetslé, Gilbert. Mouterij en Brouwerij Technologie. C.T.L. Ghent, 1984.

Boullanger, E. Malterie et Brasserie. J.B. Bailliére et Fils, Paris, 1934.

Bushness, M.E. Progress in Industrial Microbiology, Volume 19. Elsevier, Amsterdam, 1984.

Cartuyvels, Jules. Traité Complet Théorique et Pratique de la Fabrication de la Biére et du Malt. Librairie Polytechnique Jules Decq, Bruxelles, 1883.

Crombecq, Peter. Les Goûts de la Biére. Nieuwe Media Produkties bvba 2000, Antwerpen, 1985.

de Clerck, Jean. Cours de Brasserie. Louvain, 1948.

Derdelinckx G. (1987) CEREVESIA, 12, p. 153: La Refermentation de la Biére en Bouteilles.

Lense, Karl. Katechismus der Brauerie - Praxis. F.P. Datterer and Cie., Verlaganstalt , Munchen, 1940.

Malepeyre, F. Nouveau Manuel Complet du Brasseur. Encyclopedie Roret, Paris, 1896.

Trappistes et Bières d'Abbayes - Raymond Buren, 1990, Bruxelles, Glénat Bénélux.

Wilssens, Marie-Anne. Optimo Bruno Grimbergensis. Elsevier Librico, Zaventem, 1986.

Vanderstichele, Dr. G. La Brasserie de Fermentation Haute. E. Bernard, Paris, 1905.

Verlinden, H. LeerBoek der Gistings Nijverheid. 1933.

BP

BREWERS PUBLICATIONS ORDER FORM

PROFESSIONAL BREWING BOOKS

QTY.	TITLE	STOCK #	PRICE	EXT. PRICE
______	Brewery Planner	440	80.00	________
______	North American Brewers Resource Directory	445	80.00	________
______	Principles of Brewing Science	415	29.95	________

THE BREWERY OPERATIONS SERIES
from Micro and Pubbrewers Conferences

QTY.	TITLE	STOCK #	PRICE	EXT. PRICE
______	Volume 4, 1987 Conference	424	25.95	________
______	Volume 5, 1988 Conference	428	25.95	________
______	Volume 6, 1989 Conference	430	25.95	________
______	Volume 7, 1990 Conference	433	25.95	________
______	Volume 8, 1991 Conference, Brewing Under Adversity	442	25.95	________
______	Volume 9, 1992 Conference, Quality Brewing — Share the Experience	447	25.95	________

CLASSIC BEER STYLE SERIES

QTY.	TITLE	STOCK #	PRICE	EXT. PRICE
______	Pale Ale	431	11.95	________
______	Continental Pilsener	434	11.95	________
______	Lambic	437	11.95	________
______	Vienna, Märzen, Oktoberfest	444	11.95	________
______	Porter	443	11.95	________
______	Belgian Ale	446	11.95	________
______	German Wheat Beer	448	11.95	________
______	Scotch Ale	449	11.95	________
______	Bock (available Winter 1993)	452	11.95	________

BEER AND BREWING SERIES, for homebrewers and beer enthusiasts from National Homebrewers Conferences

QTY.	TITLE	STOCK #	PRICE	EXT. PRICE
______	Volume 8, 1988 Conference	427	21.95	________
______	Volume 9, 1989 Conference	429	21.95	________
______	Volume 10, 1990 Conference	432	21.95	________
______	Volume 11, 1991 Conference, Brew Free Or Die!	435	21.95	________
______	Volume 12, 1992 Conference, Just Brew It!	436	21.95	________

GENERAL BEER AND BREWING INFORMATION

QTY.	TITLE	STOCK #	PRICE	EXT. PRICE
______	Brewing Lager Beer	417	14.95	________
______	Brewing Mead	418	11.95	________
______	Dictionary of Beer and Brewing	414	19.95	________
______	Evaluating Beer	456	25.95	________
______	Great American Beer Cookbook	455	24.95	________
______	Winners Circle	407	11.95	________

SUBTOTAL ________

Colo. Residents Add 3% Sales Tax ________

P & H * ________

TOTAL ________

Call or write for a free *Beer Enthusiast* catalog today.

- U.S. funds only.
- All Brewers Publications books come with a money-back guarantee.

***Postage & Handling:** $3 for the first book ordered, plus $1 for each book thereafter. Canadian and foreign orders please add $4 for the first book and $2 for each book thereafter. Orders cannot be shipped without appropriate P&H.

Brewers Publications, PO Box 1679, Boulder, CO 80306-1679, (303) 447-0816, FAX (303) 447-2825.

BP-O93

Brewery Operations, Vol. 4

1987 Microbrewers Conference Transcript

Expert information on brewing, marketing, engineering and management. Chapters include: Malt Extract in Microbrewing • Techniques of Major Breweries • Engineering for the Microbrewer • Developing a Marketing Plan • How to Hire Good People • Equipment Systems for the Brewpub • BATF Regulations.

5 1/2 x 8 1/2, 210 pp. **Suggested retail price $25.95**

Brewery Operations, Vol. 5

1988 Microbrewers Conference Transcript

Are you a brewpub operator, just getting into the industry or thinking of expanding? Then you'll want to know every fact in *Brewery Operations, Vol. 5.* There were 21 specialized presentations (27 speakers in all) at the 1988 Conference, providing practical information for all brewers. Topics include: Brewery Feasibility Studies • Equipment Design Considerations • Franchising • Working with Distributors • Yeast Handling • Product Development • Expanding Your Brewery.

5 1/2 x 8 1/2, 330 pp. **Suggested retail price $25.95**

Brewery Operations, Vol. 6

1989 Microbrewers Conference Transcript

Your guide to the rapidly changing environment of pub- and microbreweries. Chapters include: Legislative Initiatives • Handling Regulatory Authorities • Beer Packaging Design • Working with Distributors • Quality Assurance Systems • Current Federal Regulations • Offering Other's Beers.

5 1/2 x 8 1/2, 205 pp. **Suggested retail price $25.95**

Brewery Operations, Vol. 7

1990 Microbrewers Conference Transcript

Brewery Operations, Vol. 7, the transcripts of the Denver Conference for microbrewers and pubbrewers, reviews the world of the new commercial brewer. Subjects in the published transcripts include Jeff Mendel's industry overview; Charlie Papazian's presentation on off-flavors; Fred Scheer, of Frankenmuth Brewery, on bottling; Dan Gordon, of Gordon Biersch Brewpub, on trub; Al Geitner, of Pub Brewing Co., on alternative beverages for the brewpub; John Foley, of Connecticut Brewing Co., on strategic plan for contract brewers and Dan Carey, of J.V. Northwest, on microbrewery design performance.

5 1/2 x 8 1/2, 212 pp. **Suggested retail price $25.95**

Brewing Under Adversity
Brewery Operations, Vol. 8

1991 Microbrewers Conference Transcripts

It is more difficult than ever to run a successful brewing business in today's climate of anti-alcohol sentiment and restrictive legislation. The 1991 Microbrewers Conference, titled "Brewing Under Adversity," addressed this topic and many others pertaining to the smaller brewing venture, and *Brewing Under Adversity, Brewery Operations, Vol, 8* brings this information to you. Topics include: Brewing Under Adversity, Industry Overview, Packaging for the Environment, Brewpub Design Efficiency and Operating Multiple Units.

5 1/2 x 8 1/2, 246 pp. Suggested retail price $25.95

Brewers Resource Directory

Here are the updated phone numbers, addresses, personnel and descriptions of North American breweries and suppliers you've been waiting for! We know how valuable this publication is by the thousands sold to date. It's the most definitive directory in the industry. You get complete listings for: Microbreweries and Brewpubs • Ingredient Suppliers • Brewing Consultants • Equipment Manufacturers • Large Breweries • Associations and Publications • State Laws and Excise Taxes. Updated and published yearly. Includes a revised and expanded beer styles chapter.

Plus, an informative article and statistics summarizing the year's activities and trends.

8 1/2 x 11, 281 pp. Suggested retail price $80.00

Brewery Planner

A Guide to Opening Your Own Small Brewery

When planning to open a brewery, it only makes sense to find out everything you can from those who have already learned about the business, sometimes the hard way. *Brewery Planner* is designed to prepare the new brewer for every potential obstacle or necessity. It is a collection of articles written by experienced brewers, covering The Physical Plant in Section One, Tips from the Experts in Section Two, Marketing and Distribution in Section Three, and Business Plan, Including Templates for Financial Statements in Section Four. A must for anyone planning to open a brewery.

8 1/2 x 11, 191 pp. Suggested retail price $70.00

The Winners Circle

There is no other book like it! 126 award-winning homebrew recipes for 21 styles of lager, ale, and mead.

Start brewing with this refreshing collection of tried-and-true homebrew recipes selected from the winners of the AHA National Homebrew Competition.

5 1/2 x 8 1/2, 298 pp. Suggested retail price $11.95

Principles of Brewing Science

George Fix has created a masterful look at the chemistry and biochemistry of brewing. With a helpful short course in the appendix, this book will unravel the mysteries of brewing, showing you what really goes on during the making of beer and how you can improve it. An absolute must for those who want to get the most out of their brewing.

5 1/2 x 8 1/2, 250 pp. **Suggested retail price $29.95**

Pale Ale

First in the Classic Beer Style Series

Terry Foster, a British expatriate and renowned expert on British beers has created a technical masterpiece on pale ale, the world's most popular style of ale. Written with an entertaining historical perspective, this book more than measures up to its subject matter.

Chapters include history, character, flavor, ingredients, brewing, methods and comparisons of commercial pale ales.

5 1/2 x 8 1/2, 140 pp. **Suggested retail price $11.95**

Continental Pilsener

Second in the Classic Beer Style Series

Learn the ingredients and techniques that produce this golden, distinctively hopped lager. Dave Miller, an award-winning brewer and author, takes you through the history, flavor, ingredients and methods of the beer that revolutionized brewing.

You'll also learn about current commercial examples of the style. Professionals and homebrewers alike will enjoy this exploration of a classic beer.

5 1/2 x 8 1/2, 102 pp. **Suggested retail price $11.95**

Lambic

Third in the Classic Beer Style Series

Lambic, by Jean-Xavier Guinard, is the only book ever published that completely examines this exotic and elusive style. From origins to brewing techniques, *Lambic* unravels the mysteries that make this rare style so popular. *Lambic* contains the only directory of the lambic breweries of Belgium. Guinard, a student of Dr. Michael Lewis at the University of California at Davis, grew up in the shadow of lambic breweries and combined vocation and avocation to produce this wonderful book.

5 1/2 x 8 1/2, 169 pp. **Suggested retail price $11.95**

Vienna, Märzen, Oktoberfest

Fourth in the Classic Beer Style Series

Vienna, a dark, delicious lager, has never been easier to brew. George Fix, well known homebrewer and beer scientist, and his wife, Laurie, explore the history and techniques of this style, giving recipes and in-depth instructions.

Brewers have long known that this is a difficult beer to make true to style—but *Vienna*, the first book to explore this lager, helps even beginning brewers master it.

5 1/2 x 8/12, approx. 160 pp. **Suggested retail price $11.95**

Porter

Fifth in the Classic Beer Style Series

In the mid-eighteenth century, porter was such a popular beer style that some of the fermenting vats were large enough for 100-200 people to dine in them during their inauguration. But more recently, this style was almost lost to modern beerlovers. Today porter is making a comeback, and Terry Foster brings to homebrewers the history, techniques and lore of this rich brew. Porter is the only book available on the style, and it is one of the most colorfully written and enjoyable beer style books available.

5 1/2 x 8 1/2, approx. 170 pp. **Suggested retail price $11.95**